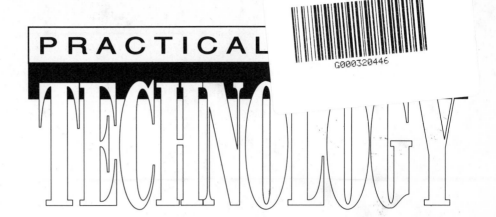

PRACTICAL TECHNOLOGY

TEACHING WITHIN THE
NATIONAL CURRICULUM

DR DOUGLAS P NEWTON AND LYNN D NEWTON

Published by Scholastic Publications Ltd,
Villiers House, Clarendon Avenue,
Leamington Spa, Warwickshire, CV32 5PR

© 1991 Scholastic Publications Ltd

Written by Dr Douglas P. Newton and Lynn D.
Newton
Edited by Frances Hubbard and Juliet Gladston
Designed by Sue Limb
Illustrated by Lynne Willey and The Drawing
Room
Photographs by Bob Bray (pp. 5, 55, 113), John
Twinning (pp. 7, 79, 139), Paul Carter (p. 23),
LEGO UK (p. 43), Chris Birchall Associates (p. 65),
Terry Williams (p. 123), Isabelle Butchinsky (pp.
147, 167), John Harris (pp. 170, 173)

Typeset by Studio Photoset, Leicester
Artwork by Norfolk House Graphic Designers,
Leicester
Printed by Ebenezer Baylis & Son, Worcester

Front cover designed by Joy White and Sue Limb
Front cover illustration by Nick Armson

The publishers wish to thank the Controller of
Her Majesty's Stationery Office, Falmer Press,
Design Council Publications and the Association
for Science Education for permission to quote
copyright material.

British Library Cataloguing in Publication Data

Newton, Douglas
   A practical guide to teaching technology within the national
   curriculum.
   I. Newton, Lynn
   607.1

   ISBN 0-590-76624-4

Contents

Introduction

This is a book about teaching technology in the primary school. It describes the nature of technology, the aims of technology education and the requirements of *Technology in the National Curriculum* but it is, above all else, a practical book and is concerned largely with classroom practice. What it says has two purposes: first, it offers information with direct classroom application, and second, through example, it tries to show how activities might be planned for the unique situation each classroom presents.

To suit these purposes, the book has been written so that most chapters can stand alone, ready for consultation. Those unfamiliar with teaching technology may choose to read it through from the beginning. Others may prefer to select those sections which meet their immediate needs.

The book has three parts. Section One concerns itself with technology education broadly; its nature, approaches, planning, assessment and recording. Section Two is more concerned with *Technology in the National Curriculum*: its interpretation and the fulfilment of its requirements. Section Three provides information on some of the key content areas of technology. It must be emphasised that the aim of this last section is to inform the teacher and not the child. From time to time, teachers on in-service courses have told us that a lack of basic knowledge in these areas has made them hesitant to develop their own ideas into practical lessons. Hopefully, these brief notes will prove useful in that respect.

Section one Teaching technology

Chapter one

Technology and technology education

The nature of technology

Without technology, we would face the elements naked and single-handed. Other animals can survive like that but the human animal is better suited to deal with the environment with the help of tools and implements and what these, and the mind, can make. Fifty thousand years ago this may have been little more than pointed sticks, sharp stones, pierced bones, cured skins and temporary shelters. Today, it is the Persian carpet, the television, the water supply system, the zip-fastener and the computer; in short, the whole panoply of human invention and ingenuity with which we insulate ourselves from the environment, amuse ourselves and supply our wants and needs.

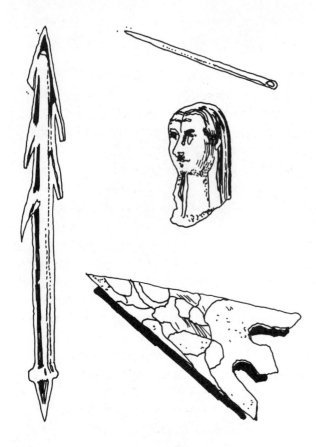

Figure 1.1   Flint arrowhead, bone figurine and needle and antler spearhead.

Figure 1.1 shows some of the artefacts used by hunter-gatherers of 20,000 years ago. Such artefacts helped them satisfy the need for food, clothing and shelter. They also made bone carvings of what were, presumably, their gods, so they must have felt other needs too.

By about 10,000 years ago, some animals had been domesticated and simple farming was practised. The nomad's camp became a semi-permanent settlement and implements evolved to meet new needs. At first, turning the sod would be a back-breaking process of pulling and pushing some form of digging stick or plough until, by at least 3500 BC, the ox was harnessed to it. Instead of the light-weight tent, it was now worth building substantial and durable shelters. Food was cooked on permanent

hearths, stores laid up for winter and various textiles woven. Surpluses might be transported to the emerging cities and bartered on market stalls while lords and priests levied taxes and devised systems for collecting and recording payments.

Figure 1.2   Pot bowl and flint sickle blade of the early farmer.

Even in the dim past, the aim of technology was not unlike that of its modern counterpart. It generated *artefacts*, for example, clothing (by 50,000 BC), the wheeled cart (by 3200 BC), and the sickle (by 3000 BC). In addition, it created *systems* such as the bow and arrow (by 30,000 BC) and the canal (about 4000 BC). It made *environments*, like the sun-dried clay brick building (by 6000 BC) – all, in the final analysis, to satisfy human *needs*. Technology was also directed towards extending the abilities of the human body through simple machines like the lever, and by harnessing the power of stronger animals, and that of the wind and of fire.

Technology remains concerned with *extending human capabilities*, both physical, as in space exploration, and mental, with the computer. *Knowledge of materials*, their properties and how to work them, is essential if technology is to be effective. Early man demonstrated this in knapping flint, polishing stone, drilling bone, weaving baskets and textiles, and in reinforcing mud bricks with straw. At the same time, the early products of technology were improved as new materials were discovered and knowledge was extended. Our ancestors were not averse to making their own materials when it was worth their while. *Lapis lazuli*, a rare and highly prized mineral for jewellery, was being simulated in the Near East 6000 years ago and the earliest known plywood dates from 2800 BC, in Egypt.

Figure 1.3   Early, Roman and recent oil lamps.

Technological capability developed over succeeding millennia. The testimony to Greek and Roman building technology, for instance, is that so much of it still stands.

These buildings owe their longevity to some knowledge of materials and structural engineering rather than to a blind faith in placing one massive block on another. The seven great sights of the Ancient World are testaments to the Ancients' ability to create giant compressive structures – the Pyramid at Giza, the Hanging Gardens of Babylon, the statue of Zeus at Olympia, the Colossus of Rhodes, the Temple of Artemis at Ephesos, the Mausoleum at Halicarnassus, and the Pharos lighthouse at Alexandria. At least for the rich, buildings did not lack the creature comforts we take for granted today. They had underfloor heating, hot water on tap and drainage systems. There even exists a design for an air-bed made of animal skins. At least 90 per cent of energy needs was supplied by plants, animals and people (often slaves). However, the energy of wind and moving water was also tapped through the use of the sailing boat and the water-wheel. It was during this time that the water-wheel was improved, force pumps were constructed and simple machines, such as the crane (described by a Roman about 2000 years ago) were widely used. However, some of this technological capability was lost in the contraction of the Roman Empire so that visitors to Charlemagne in AD 807 were able to astonish the court with a water clock, albeit an elaborate one. Yet this was not the case with the water-wheel and windmill which continued to spread and develop during the Renaissance.

Figure 1.4   The Pharos lighthouse.

The decline of slavery, the decimation of the population by plagues and the opportunity for feudal lords to make money, are some of the reasons given for the improvement and spread of wind and water driven machinery. They were used for all sorts of tasks: sawing wood, fulling cloth, making paper, as well as grinding corn. As Europe came out of the Middle Ages, other notable inventions were the collar harness for horses which increased the efficiency of the heavy, wheeled plough (by the eleventh century), printing with moveable type (Gutenberg, 1438, but used in China 400 years earlier), the mechanical clock (about AD 1290), and the firearm (about AD 1350).

The scientific revolution of the seventeenth century provided technology with a structured body of knowledge and a way of working so that, according to popular perceptions, it became 'the appliance of science'. In the past, there were itinerant, bridge-building monks and military engineers such as Leonardo da Vinci but their flights of fancy were firmly contained by the materials available to them and the ways and means of working those materials. During the Industrial Revolution (about 1780 to 1850) the trickle of inventions turned into a flood. Many fell by the wayside but others led to the accoutrements of modern life which we take for granted – the aircraft, the electric iron, the telephone, the refrigerator, the pneumatic tyre, the ball-point pen, and so on. The great prime mover of the Industrial Revolution was the steam engine, a source of power independent of the vagaries of wind and water, free of the needs of people and animals and powerful beyond belief. Technology had satisfied needs; now technologists sought opportunities to use their skills in return for financial reward.

This ethos permeates modern technology. A need or *opportunity for applying technology* is perceived, knowledge and know-how are brought to bear on it, perhaps supported by research, designs are created, prototypes made and tested, modified, retested, and a product offered to the market. This is not to say that technology as an activity is a straightforward procedure, for no creative

activity can be reduced to a formula. These stages are more like landfalls on the way to a solution. Technologists must have a capacity for imagination and ingenuity, often coupled with a willingness to suspend belief in what is popularly held to be possible. None of these is totally susceptible to prescription.

The ability to invent and make is a capacity which has helped humans to survive. It is this same capacity which has made it possible to dominate the environment and extend the limited capabilities of the human body. But each new capability changes things, sometimes imperceptibly and sometimes radically. The paper-clip, made in Germany in 1900, may have done little more than displace the pin, but the petrol engine (1885) changed the environment, work, leisure and perceptions of distance. The zip-fastener (1891) may have merely replaced the button, but the mechanical clock (about 1290, for calling monks to their devotions) has enabled life's activities to be highly organised, structured and efficiently controlled.

Whether the consequences of a particular innovation are desirable is a matter for debate. Change is not always for the better and we must often abandon one thing to gain something else. We often forget, however, that there *is* a choice. Technology makes things possible but because something is possible does not mean that it has to be. Or is human nature such that what can be, will be? Our technological capability has reached the level where this is no idle question.

Technology is about satisfying human, material needs. The variety of such needs is enormous and technology must draw on a wide range of knowledge to satisfy them. Often, this knowledge comes from science, but technology is not science, although it must concern itself with science.

In satisfying a need, the prime concern is to create an effective solution, that is, something which works. However, function is seldom the only concern; what it looks, feels, sounds, smells, and tastes like, also

figure in a technologist's thinking, as does a knowledge of the properties of materials and the craft skills to work them. The sum of these concerns is still less than technology. Ultimately, technology's identity stems from its intent and that is to satisfy material needs. When we look at a product of human endeavour, it is sometimes difficult to decide whether that which gave rise to it was altogether science, art, craft, or technology. After the event, the creator's intent may be obscure; was the picture created in an act of pure self-expression, or was it assembled to cover the crack in the wall? In science, the primary intention is to understand nature; in art, the goal is self-expression; in craft, it is manufacture; in technology, it is *to design and make a product to satisfy a material need.* Each has its school curriculum counterpart and while technology education is not the same as any one, or even the total of, the others, it must concern itself with all of them.

Chronology of inventions

Before	250,000 BC	Axe
About	200,000 BC	Pit traps
About	45,000 BC	Spear
About	30,000 BC	Bow and arrow, flint knives, barbed hooks
About	10,000 BC	Farming
About	8000 BC	Comb, hammers with hafts
Before	6000 BC	Sun-baked bricks
About	4000 BC	The navigation canal (Mesopotamia)
Before	3500 BC	Ox-drawn plough, wheeled cart (Mesopotamia)
About	3000 BC	Soap (Mesopotamia), saw (Egypt), sickle
Before	2000 BC	Ball (Egypt and Persia), bronze mirror, armour
About	1400 BC	Glass bottle (Egypt)
About	1000 BC	Scissors (Egypt)
Before	700 BC	Aqueduct (Middle East)
Before	100 BC	Water-mill (Greece)
About	AD 650	Windmill (Persia)
	AD 1504	Pocket-watch
	AD 1550	Nuts and bolts
About	AD 1795	Pencil
	AD 1800	Dry battery

	AD 1827	Camera for permanent photographs
	AD 1837	Electric motor
	AD 1846	Sewing machine
	AD 1870	Barbed wire
	AD 1876	Telephone
	AD 1881	Electric torch
	AD 1885	Motor car
	AD 1891	Zip-fastener
	AD 1892	Vacuum flask
	AD 1894	Radio
	AD 1901	Vacuum cleaner
	AD 1906	Electric washing machine
	AD 1923	Electric kettle
	AD 1927	Television
About	AD 1930	Ball-point pen (Biro)
	AD 1934	Cats' eyes
	AD 1958	Video-tape recorder, laser
	AD 1962	Electronic watch
	AD 1966	Sandwich toaster
	AD 1971	Pocket calculator
	AD 1973	Whole-body scanner
	AD 1976	Concorde – first supersonic airliner
	AD 1978	Calculator watch
	AD 1981	Space shuttle
	AD 1990	Suckerball

Why teach technology?

The mere existence of technology is not, in itself, enough to justify its inclusion in the school curriculum. Only a fraction of children will grow up to become professional technologists, so we cannot argue that we must prepare them for a career in technology. Therefore, why teach it?

• First, the human ability to invent and make is instrumental in making our world what it is and what we are. In a very real way, we live in an artificial world, surrounded by the products of mind and hand. Even much of the countryside, its fields and hedgerows, is man-made. Thousands of years of inventing has filled all our lives with artefacts, systems and environments and everyone should be aware of it. An understanding of the products of technology helps us, therefore, to understand our artificial environment.

• Second, the skills and processes deployed and the traits encouraged in technology are of general value in dealing with life's material problems. These may seem minor when compared with those faced by the professional technologist, but they help people to deal effectively with their environment and take control of their lives.

• Third, since technology impinges on us all, an awareness of its nature and ways of working helps us to understand the technological society in which we live and take rational decisions regarding it. Our technological capability can be beneficial, benign, or detrimental, and sometimes more than one of these at once. Two hundred thousand years ago, one man shaping an axe and relieving himself near his shelter was of little consequence. Today, the industrial waste and refuse of two million people, wisely removed from a city by courtesy of technology, can create an off-shore disaster. Everyone needs to be aware that the use of technology can have unexpected ramifications as well as more obvious benefits. At the same time, decisions should be humane. Technology insulates us from the environment and often from one another. Face to face contact is reduced by the search for more efficient modes of transaction of which the cash dispenser and ticket-vending machine are examples. The danger is that we begin to see one another as we do these machines, failing to allow for human frailty and the human condition, and applying technological solutions to people without humanity.

• Fourth, in a technological society, technology education can have a vocational value. Where the dependence on technology is great, there will be both a need and an opportunity for those with some expertise in it.

These four reasons for teaching technology imply that we teach some of technology's *products*, some of its *processes*, and something about its *impact* and the *choices* it brings, each to a degree appropriate to the age and ability of the children.

The first three of these – the need for an understanding of the nature of technology and its impact on our lives, the general utility of technology's skills, processes and

attitudes, and preparation for life in a democratic, technological society – seem very cogent reasons for including technology in the primary school curriculum. Technology education is not about vocational training but the realities of life mean that, in the long run, the last reason is also important.

As far as the products and processes of technology are concerned, the National Curriculum makes it clear that it is to be the processes which are central: **'Design and Technology is about identifying needs, generating ideas, planning, making and testing . . . [and it] is a subject concerned with practical action [aimed at solving] practical problems'**. It warns that following patterns and working to prescribed designs **'. . . is not Design and Technology'** (*National Curriculum: Non Statutory Guidance: Design and Technology*).

Children doing technology

Certain aspects of technology may have been taught in some schools under various guises for many years: for example, technology from the past, model-making, the safe and effective use of some cutting and shaping tools, ways of fixing materials together, and a consideration of aesthetics. However, whatever guise it appears in, technology education is *not* merely about the acquisition of craft skills, experience of working with one or two materials, or the ability to follow a pattern. It is less constrained and offers the child genuine opportunities for creativity. In the primary school, working 'like a technologist' is practised, but this cannot happen in a vacuum. Knowledge and know-how from a wide range of sources support the activity.

The following are taken from real examples of children doing technology in the classroom and are based on case studies made by Yvonne Christine Curtis, Val Durkin, Margaret Hinshelwood and Lorna Ternent. They highlight some aspects that you will need to be aware of and point out some pitfalls.

Case study 1

The first study is of children in Year 1 (five-to six-year-olds) of the infant school. The stimulus for this technological activity was a class visit to the local playground where the apparatus was made from logs which had been fixed together with bolts. Two girls, Ann and Jane, and two boys, Robert and Mark, were observed in detail. After some play, the children's discussion was guided towards the materials, the way they were joined together, and the function of the parts. They recognised that wood was used and that the ends of the logs were driven into the ground so that they would not fall down, but they lacked the vocabulary to describe how the pieces were joined. This what they said:

Ann: It's stuck.
Robert: It's got bits in there.
Jane: It's metal.
Robert: The bits of metal go down the holes.
Mark: There, they're nails.

Faced with this difficulty, they supplemented their explanation by pointing to the bits concerned. This was demonstrated again in the classroom when talking about the swing.

Robert: At the top it's got some squares and it's just all wonky, so it's loose, so it can swing.
Jane: It's got chains and it's fastened on to some metal and some wood.
Mark: And you can stand up and you can swing on it when you hold on to the metal bits and the string.
Ann: Well, there's knobs at the top and they're slack.

The structure of the see-saw, roundabout and slide were described similarly, but it was in describing the slide that the children resorted to using their hands most frequently. Hands were used to indicate the angle of the slide, the slippery surface and, by firm pressure between hands, the rigidity of the structure.

For those devices which moved, the children showed an appreciation that a force was needed and that someone had to provide it. For instance, in connection with the swing:

Robert: You push it. You have to push it.
Mark: Push with your feet.
Robert: Or you could use your feet going up and down.
Jane: Or you can get a person to push you.

When asked if the roundabout could work by itself, the children expressed amusement. There was no doubt that an external agent was needed.

The children were invited to think of ways of making the playground better. There were a lot of ideas and many were impractical, but there were some which could be developed further. From these, the children were asked to select one they would like to make as a model and draw how it would look. All were conservative and chose familiar playground apparatus, but they differed in the method of construction. Ann's was to be a swing made from cardboard, Robert's was a roundabout made with plastic Meccano, Jane chose a swing to be made with LEGO, and Mark wanted to make a roundabout from junk material.

Contrary to the teacher's expectation, the designing stage was engaged upon with interest and enthusiasm. Ann was clear how she would proceed; she drew the components of her swing on card and cut them out. Making matching pieces gave rise to a false start as she tried to measure and draw with a ruler. Eventually, she abandoned this approach and used the cut pieces as templates. She was not up to the task of fixing the seat to its suspension threads and needed the teacher to suggest an effective method. Help was also needed in tying the knots.

Jane's LEGO swing had two supporting pillars, bridged across the top, all patiently and methodically assembled. The seat again was a problem and the teacher had to show her how it might be suspended from the cross-bar.

Robert's Meccano roundabout had an open box on each end of a strip. The strip was pivoted at the centre, rather like a set of scales, and was free to rotate about that point. Unfortunately, the strip was too flexible and the boxes tended to catch on the base. With assistance, this was corrected by raising the supporting pillar.

Mark's junk roundabout involved some searching for the 'right bits'. In essence, the design was similar to that of Robert's, but Mark did not make provision for the rotation of the turntable. He needed a lot of help to overcome this difficulty which he did by using a nail as a spindle.

At this stage, all of the models seemed to work well but the children were required to test them with a small doll. Ann found that its weight was too much for her card swing: 'The legs are too short and it keeps falling over. It needs to have stronger legs'. On Robert's roundabout the doll's weight again made the box catch on the base: 'That bit there is too bendy. I need to make it firmer, like that.' Jane's swing proved to be too small to accommodate the doll and Mark's roundabout was unable to take its weight.

The teacher suggested that they might like to make an improved model. The children were enthusiastic but wanted to work in pairs. This seemed to inject sufficient novelty to motivate them again. This time, the girls chose cardboard tubes for the uprights of their swing and an egg box lid for the seat. With the teacher's help, they decided to use a piece of dowel as the cross-bar. The boys' roundabout comprised a cone on which rotated a shallow, open cylinder, divided into sections for seats. These models worked well and there was evident pride in the outcome. However, only the girls showed interest in making the model attractive by decorating it.

From this case study it can be seen that very young children are able to engage in worthwhile technological activity. Although a lack of vocabulary may conceal their understanding, non-verbal communication may indicate a far greater appreciation. For example, the children in this case study

were shown to have appreciated that a slide is a system of related parts, each with a function.

Many teachers expect designing and planning to be seen by children as rather tedious chores, but these children did not. Here, the teacher made these stages almost ends in themselves and not time-consuming precursors to the main event. Presented in this way, as was evaluation of the project, they received an appropriate amount of attention.

Lack of experience and manipulative skill meant that the teacher had to help and guide the children on occasions. The fruits of that assistance were apparent in the competent model making which followed the evaluation. At the same time, the exercise showed that even young children can exhibit persistence and patience in problem solving.

Case study 2

Fred, Carl, Norma and Lisa were in Year 3 (seven- to eight-year-olds); they were industrious, well-motivated, and able to work in a group. The technological activity arose from a topic on the Stone Age, the task being to make a wooden Stone-Age artefact. This was a novel material for the children to work with and they therefore needed to be briefly instructed on shaping it and safe tool handling.

Fred chose to make a model spear, Norma a model canoe, Lisa a model of a handcart, and Carl a model of an animal-drawn cart.

Lisa: The sandpaper makes it go really smooth.

Carl: The sand-stick makes the wood raggy.

Lisa: Look at the dust when you blow.

Norma: You get tons of chips out of the canoe, don't you?

Fred: The drill makes a hole quick. I thought it would take ages.

Norma: The round sand-stick is great – it makes round bits. It's easier to saw than the cardboard for the boat.

Fred: I'll have to shape a flint to get a pointy bit. That looks really good now. I'll paint it grey to look like a flint.

Carl: We could make flints out of clay.

Fred: No, but if we banged them they'd break to bits.

Carl: No, they need to be stiff.

These activities are very different to those carried out by the children in Year 1. Here they served to widen the children's experience of the properties and working of new materials which they would be able to use in more open problem-solving activities later. This would not, of course, be the only teaching strategy. If it was, the children

Figure 1.5 Making a canoe from balsa.

would not have opportunities to perceive needs and to design artefacts, systems and environments to fulfil those needs, using whatever materials were appropriate. The discussion between the children illustrates how they learned about the properties of new materials and the capabilities of the tools as they worked them. It was noted in the first case study that some of the Year 1 children showed little interest in aesthetic embellishment. In this instance, however, all took care over the appearance of the finished objects, but Fred's comment, 'That looks really good now', suggests that the concern was purely for a realistic appearance.

Case study 3

Emma, Susan, Rajeev and Irvin were in Year 5 (nine- to ten-year-olds) when they were introduced to forces and their uses in a sequence of four lessons designed to illustrate what a force is, friction as a force, and the use of force to move an elastic band powered roller. They were then asked to design and make a vehicle which would carry a LEGO man at least 30cm. This could have led them to examine toy cars, LEGO vehicles, and other potential solutions to the problem, but the four did not spend much time on such research. They were too eager to start. Similarly, their sketches were incomplete and showed little forethought about a source of power for the vehicles. The children had already had some experience of making structures with centimetre square section jelutong so they successfully made their vehicles, but were unable to make them move under their own power. Attempts at using elastic bands to propel them also failed. All four lost interest in the project and abandoned their models.

This study is particularly interesting because this particular exercise is usually considered appropriate for children of this age, but here it failed miserably. Ways of propelling a vehicle seem fairly obvious to us because we have accumulated a reservoir of relevant knowledge and know-how. We readily recall such things as elastic band propelled aeroplanes and

balloon driven toys. Children, on the other hand, may have played with such things, but do not always appreciate the nature of the 'special bits' – the mechanisms which enable action to take place. Here, they knew a little of energy and how to make a buggy, but nothing about ways and means of bringing the two together. They had two of the components of a solution but not the third. Unfortunately, given a problem, children often want to press on with the making of the solution and learning about energy storage and its controlled release gets in the way of that. Any problem needs

to be analysed carefully into its prerequisite knowledge and skills components and provision made for acquiring these effectively before or as they are needed.

Invention cannot occur in a vacuum. Children need to bring their existing knowledge and know-how to bear on the problem in hand. When the requisite knowledge and skills are absent or inadequate, satisfactory solutions are less likely, interest evaporates and involvement becomes dispirited and erratic.

Case study 4

Four children from Year 6 (ten- to eleven-year-olds) were at the focus of this study. The opportunity for technology presented itself through plans for a charity fund-raising event and the class had decided to

make games and use them in a fun-fair. Three of the group were confident and intelligent and co-operated successfully to make a game with an electrical buzzer, a Grand Prix race track, and a pin-ball machine. The fourth, Ben, deserves particular attention. Ben had serious learning problems, disliked any form of writing, seldom completed tasks, whatever they were, and was a low achiever, lacking in confidence and self-esteem. He was also sometimes aggressive and lonely.

Ben's first problem was that he could not find anyone willing to work with him. As everyone else was engaged upon tasks to do with the project, Ben may have felt obliged to do likewise. His first idea was to make a version of 'pin the tail on the donkey'. He drew a large face and provided eyes, nose, mouth, and ears to be pinned on it. Unfortunately, those who tested it were less than enthusiastic. Ben was very disappointed and it took time and teacher support to bring him to start again.

Ben's second attempt was to make a version of blow football in which pingpong balls were to be blown around an obstacle course of yoghurt pots which had been stuck to card. He became interested in the task and spent a lot of time, including his spare time, perfecting the design. He devised a scoring system, had the game tested and was gratified when it was well-received. Ben saw the need to make the game attractive to others and he decorated it, made a poster advertising it, drew a large diagram and provided a key to its parts.

Ben's self-esteem seemed to be enhanced by his success and his ability to take appropriate decisions himself. In the opinion of his teacher, 'in terms of personal achievement, his is probably the best success story'. Just as children of all ages can develop their technological capability, so also can children of all abilities.

Some children showed a lack of concern for an attractive appearance. This should not be confused with a concern for realism, as in the spear-making activity in the second case study where the child seemed to be more concerned with making it look like the real thing and with role play than with aesthetic qualities. The actual appearance of an artefact may be less important to such children than the imagined qualities which they endow it with in play. Yet, faced with a real, *external* need for something to look attractive, Ben in Year 6 did so. This suggests that a concern for aesthetics might be developed by including activities of this kind in teaching schemes.

These four short case studies illustrate that technological capability is an orchestration of process skills which need to be practised together to solve problems. This does not mean that particular skills and strategies need not be practised independently, but it is important that they should be practised in concert if their essential interdependence is to make itself apparent and facility in technology as an activity is to develop adequately.

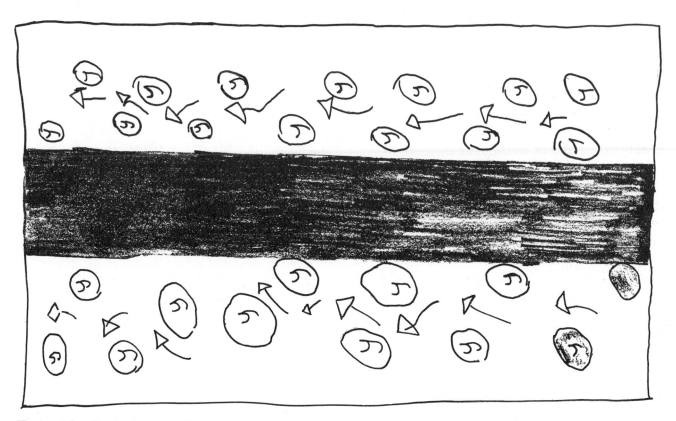

Figure 1.6   Ben's diagram of his game.

Chapter two

Developing and using design technology capability

The main staging posts of technology as a way of working are generally described as:
• see a need or opportunity;
• design an artefact, system, or environment;
• plan and make the artefact, system, or environment;
• evaluate it.

Seeing needs and opportunities

'Pupils should be able to identify and state clearly needs and opportunities for design and technological activities through investigation of the contexts of home, school, recreation, community, business and industry' (*Technology in the National Curriculum*, AT1).

Children, like many adults, will accept situations of need and live with them. Sometimes, they simply do not perceive the need or recognise the problem. At other times, they do not see needs and problems as opportunities for creative invention and problem solving on their part. Children need to be given experiences which will help them to develop the capacity to identify needs and opportunities for using technology. This means, for example, watching for situations which occur in the normal course of classroom events. A table collapses on poor Claire, pinning her to the floor; the headteacher has once again tripped over the curled up carpet, breaking her nose. These spontaneous events present the children with readily-perceived opportunities for technological problem solving which they see as being very relevant.

Of course, useful events do not always occur spontaneously when they are needed, so they have to be engineered. Your carrier bag just happens to burst as you enter the classroom; you are teaching about the Romans so you take the chance to do some technology on arches and bridge building; you arrange a visit with infants to the local playground and then do some work about playground equipment. You might choose to develop a theme from a technological starting point, as with the topic of wheels, for instance. The useful thing about these is that most have something to offer children of all ages. The need or opportunity each presents is interpreted according to the children's experiences and capabilities and they design and make accordingly. To illustrate the point, consider the following engineered situation:

A display unit has been delivered to your classroom. It was in a large, cardboard box ($1\frac{1}{2}$m cube) which now stands empty in the middle of the room. The box is too big for easy handholds. What can we do about it?

Faced with this, some children may use rollers to move the box; others may slide toys under it and push the box on to them.

Those with more experience may lift the box with a lever and slip ropes underneath so it can be carried by four people, each on the end of a rope.

Here is another situation:

You have lots of pencils in your desk/bag but you can never find what you want. Things always seem to be in a jumble.

Some children might design and make a tray with separate compartments from junk and cardboard. Others might prefer a pot made from a broad tube, sticking it to a hardboard base to make it stable, while others might design a fabric pencil case and fasten it with a nylon tape like Velcro, buttons, press studs, or laces, each according to how they perceive the need and what they see as a satisfactory solution.

Another scenario might be:

In wet weather, almost everyone arrives in wellington boots. The wet, dripping pile of boots tends to be a nuisance at times.

Young children could suggest standing the boots on the doormat which might well be satisfactory if no one is likely to fall over them. Others might feel that some sort of drip tray is needed, while older ones, being aware that it is difficult to carry a tray of

water without spilling it, might see a tilted, self-draining drip tray as the solution.

Here are some other situations which may lend themselves to perceiving needs and opportunities. Each could be followed by the prompt: 'What can we do about it?'

• Your grandmother has arthritis in her hands and has difficulty holding a cup.

• The school is closed for a fortnight and no one wants to take home the heavy, potted plant in the corner of the classroom.

• You are in trouble again for leaving your pyjamas on the bedroom floor.

Bigger problems might be presented by:

• Jack and Jill went up the hill, to fetch a pail of water . . ..

• On the way to school, you are shipwrecked on a desert island.

Surveys are also a useful way of highlighting needs and opportunities, for example:

• Results of a Year 1 survey of the toys infant children like best:

Name	Puppet	Ball	Jigsaw	Car	Paints
Bill					•
Susan	•				
Ann			•		
Rajeev	•				
Ben	•				
Yu Chen				•	
Gillian				•	
Mark		•			

Teacher: Which toy does the class like best? Most want the puppet, but we have only one in the toy box. What shall we do?

• Results of a Year 5 survey of games for wet playtimes:

Games our class like to play	How many like them?	How many are there in the wet day box?
Board games with dice	5	10
Indoor bat and ball	10	2
Blowball games	7	0
Card games	2	8
Target games	8	1
Quizzes	1	5

Teacher: Is everyone happy with this? What can we do about it?

Designing

'Pupils should be able to generate a design specification, explore ideas to produce a design proposal and develop it into a realistic, appropriate and achievable design' *(Technology in the National Curriculum,* **AT2***).*

Children must learn that there are often several solutions to a problem and that their first thoughts are not necessarily the best. They should be encouraged to develop the habit of generating more than one design and of considering each design's relative merits. This process should lead to the selection, on good grounds, of 'a realistic, appropriate and achievable design'. It obviously helps the children if the task is structured to their precise needs in respect of age, ability and experience. This can be achieved by using a designing sheet, an example of which is shown in Figure 2.1.

Technology Designing sheet

Write a sentence describing the problem which needs solving.

....

....

Make quick drawings of your ideas for solving the problem. You must have more than one idea.

1.	2.	3.
Materials needed	Materials needed	Materials needed
Tools needed	Tools needed	Tools needed

Choose your best idea. Why is it the best one?

....

Draw a good picture of the best idea. Try to make it look right. Label all the parts.

PICTURE

MATERIALS What?	NEEDED How much?

Figure 2.1 A technology design sheet.

Teachers often find that children show little interest in *designing*. They want to go straight to the *making* stage and, having attempted that (often badly), they abandon the project. It has already been shown in Chapter One that this is helped if designing is not presented as a preliminary chore, like setting the table before eating a meal. Make it a worthwhile activity in its own right. An appropriate designing sheet, varied from time to time, helps to maintain interest. It may be necessary to rein back the urge to rush through the designing stage yourself, by concealing your long-term intention, for example: '*If* you were to make a mask, what would it look like? How would you keep it on? Draw your ideas and tell me about them' or '*If* you were to make a toy that could move by itself, what would it look like? What would make it move? Draw some of your ideas and we'll have a look at them . . . What will that one do? How is the end of the elastic band fastened? What would you use to make that bit? Does it really have to be *gold* wire?' and so on. This underlines the importance of designing, makes it a worthwhile task, and reduces the risk of disappointment with the overall project.

Planning and making

'Pupils should be able to make artefacts, systems and environments, preparing and working to a plan and identifying, managing and using appropriate resources, including knowledge and processes' *(Technology in the National Curriculum, AT3).*

The outcome of the designing stage is often a sketch of an *artefact*, a *system*, or an *environment*. These can be defined as:
• artefacts – objects made by people, for example, a spoon, a money belt, a swing ;
• systems – sets of objects or activities which together perform a task, for example, a bicycle, a drawbridge, a house, a programme for running a fête, the National Grid for distributing electricity ;
• environments – surroundings made or

developed by people, for example, a playground, a shopping complex, a park.

Sometimes, the product has a flavour of more than one of these categories, for instance, an operating theatre is a system *and* an environment and is full of artefacts.

The designing sheet, given as an example previously, also includes some elements of planning with regard to the nature and quantity of the materials needed, but it could be extended to include others, especially those relating to the sequence of events in making something. We might, for instance, add 'What part will you make first?' and extend the list until the child has described the making sequence. With some things, the sequence of making and joining is crucial. Having made a buggy and all its superstructure, the child may find that there is now no way of fitting the proposed means of propulsion. Even with forethought it is easy to be caught out, but experience is a good teacher.

There are other aspects of planning which need to be considered from time to time. Some tasks will be co-operative ventures. Infants might make models for an adventure playground or juniors might be working on the rolling stock for a railway company, and for both these tasks, there has to be agreement on the scale of things. A cardboard figure to represent an average-size person is a useful aid here. There must also be some agreement on who makes what; it would be an unusual playground or railway if everyone made slides or engines. Other tasks may be designed to introduce the economic aspects of technology. The materials could be given price tags and the children given a spending limit. Unless they cost their designs, they could end up bankrupt. A designing sheet with a cost column added to the 'materials needed' table would focus attention on that.

Finally, the children are ready to make their designs. Many materials may be used. Some will be determined by the task and the teacher, others will be more open. Children need to choose and work with appropriate materials. Some of this knowledge and know-how may come from other areas of the curriculum, but a lot will come from using a wide range of materials in technology. Inevitably, there are limits to

resources which may mean that children are obliged to work with only one or two materials. This will inhibit what they can make, what success they can have, and what they learn.

Children need to have the opportunity to work with a *range* of materials to make *progress* in their ability to use them. This needs thought, planning and an awareness of the potential and limitations of working with particular materials. Of course, while one material might be at the focus of an activity, others are commonly used with it, especially in fixing the parts together. Working with various materials is discussed at length later in this chapter.

Evaluating

'Pupils should be able to develop, communicate and act upon an evaluation of the processes, products and effects of their design and technological activities and of those of others, including those from other times and cultures'
(Technology in the National Curriculum, AT4).

Children need experience in making and discussing judgements about the quality of products: how well they are suited to their purpose, how aesthetically pleasing they are, and whether or not they are good value. In part, this can be developed through separate evaluation exercises, but it is also important to turn the feeling of dissatisfaction or exultation experienced when a child makes something into a coherent and reasoned comment. This can be achieved by careful questioning: 'Does it work?', 'Which part is the best?', 'Why do you like that the most?', 'I like that, why don't you?' and 'Could you make it work better?'

Sometimes it is appropriate to take the results of such an evaluation and make a new, improved artefact. This can be a boring exercise if it is nothing more than 'doing corrections', and therefore some variation needs to be introduced. It can often be sufficient merely to alter the groups or to change from individual to paired work. Another strategy is to alter the task slightly so that, for example, in making a drawbridge for a castle, the drawbridge is replaced by a portcullis. Both tasks have design problems in common and the evaluation of one is akin to the designing, planning and making of the other. Occasionally, it is also possible to vary the task by changing the material.

Evaluation is not an exercise which is confined to what the children make. They should also have the chance to evaluate technological products from earlier times, from different cultures, and from the commercial world. While few will become design engineers, all will be users of artefacts, systems, and environments and they should be prepared to compare products effectively. The following are some examples of this kind of evaluation; the process is essentially the same as that used in appraising the children's own work.

Comparisons (for younger children):
• A child tries out several spades in the sand pit and chooses the best one.

• A child finds the best, general purpose bag.

Figure 2.3   The 'best shopping bag' problem.

• A child is sent to collect a book which is just out of reach.

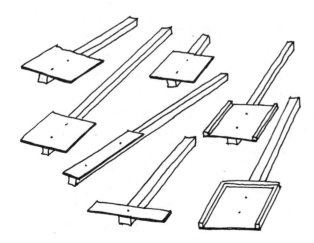

Figure 2.2   A range of simple spades made from hardboard nailed to wooden handles.

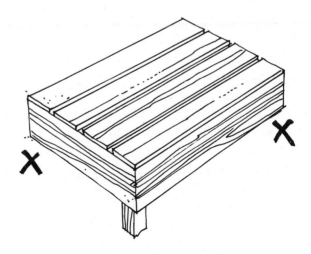

Figure 2.4   The rocking 'tomato box' stool problem. Legs xx are shortened and the box generally strengthened to take a child's weight.

Comparisons (for older children):
• Old and new tin-openers.
• A plastic bottle and a waxed card carton used to hold milk.
• An early propelling pencil and a recent one.
• Horse transport and motor transport.
• Earth lavatories and water closets.

Opportunities for such comparisons often arise naturally, in the course of work in history, environmental studies and from a story.

History

The nineteenth century was an age of inventions: modes of transport, the telephone, various labour-saving devices, and many more which fell by the wayside. Children often do not think that what is commonplace for them was once invented – for instance, the ball-point pen, the propelling pencil, and the clock – and that there was a time when they did not exist. Discussion of what life was like before the motor car, television, toilets, wellington boots, and electricity, helps them to see the impact which technology has had on their lives. Those inventions that did not make it are also instructive since they provide the opportunity for technological evaluation. Two examples follow:

• What did people use before the vacuum cleaner was invented?

Figure 2.5   A hand-operated vacuum cleaner of about 1900. How does it compare with a modern one?

• Why did this invention not catch on?

Figure 2.6   An electrically-powered bicycle, taking electricity from and running on overhead wires.

Environmental studies

While history is likely to be part of a broader environmental studies programme, other aspects of such studies also lend themselves to technological evaluation. For example, when visiting a farm, children might compare the various ways of containing animals (fence, hedge and hurdles) with regard to effectiveness and appearance. A study of a shopping precinct, on the other hand, might lead to the evaluation of the effectiveness of shop signs or provision of seating for the infirm.

Using a story

Su Tung's new chopsticks

When Su Tung was small, she had been given a pair of ivory chopsticks that she was very proud of. But one day, when she was watching television, she saw that ivory came from elephants' tusks. With horror, she realised that an elephant had been killed to make her chopsticks! Su Tung decided it was wrong to have ivory chopsticks. Why should an elephant die just so that she could have something with which to pick up her food? She would never use them again!

Su Tung had no money and therefore was unable to buy new chopsticks, so she decided to make some. Things to use were easy to find; there were straws, smooth white sticks, bright brass rods, and clear plastic tubes. All seemed just right. Which was she to use?

A suitable display of straws, pieces of dowel, metal rods and the empty tubes from ball-point pens should be available for the evaluation. The story can be adapted to suit the materials available and the children should be pressed to give rational reasons for their choice. The use of stories in teaching technology is considered more fully in Chapter Ten.

While there will be times when it might be appropriate to focus on one of these stages, children should generally have a number of opportunities to use them as a complete package. This does not mean that the path has, by necessity, to be from need to evaluation. It may be, for example, that some existing artefact is found wanting, as with the wobbly tomato box described above (Figure 2.4). Discussion about its shortcomings (evaluation) leads to a perception of a need and the design of something which satisfies that need better than the tomato box, through planning and making to the evaluation of the new product.

These four staging posts – identifying needs, designing, planning and making, and evaluating – have been presented in a logical sequence but, of course, the process of invention is not necessarily a step-by-step one, completing stage one, then stage two, and so on. In practice, tentative ideas might be lightly sketched and explored with many forward and backward steps between the stages as thoughts become progressively firmer. It may be nearer the truth to say that, while progress is forward through the stages, there are often second, third, and even further thoughts.

Working with materials

Junk materials

By junk materials, we mean a collection of diverse objects. In practice, this tends to consist of packaging from the home and the school: pop bottles, shoe boxes, yoghurt pots, margarine cartons and so on. It should be distinguished from similar objects collected for their material content, rather than the shape, transparency, or some similar attribute. Thus, it does not include cardboard boxes which are to be cut into card sheets, or margarine cartons which will be cut into plastic rectangles. Here the objects are used to supplement the stock of card and plastics, respectively, and these materials are discussed in the appropriate sections below. The materials for junk technology have been collected because they look useful as they are. Bottle tops make good wheels, bobbins serve as pulleys and a shoe box will make a chassis, a model house, a doll's bed, a temporary home for a pet, the head of a robot, a post box, and innumerable other artefacts.

Teaching technology with junk materials has some advantages, not least being that they are readily available and cost very little beyond what is needed to fix the bits together. From the children's point of view, they have the chance to work with a wide range of materials and may make a large number of artefacts successfully. Direct manipulation of the ready-made shapes can stimulate a child's imagination and help to formulate a design in a concrete way. Most junk materials may be cut with a junior

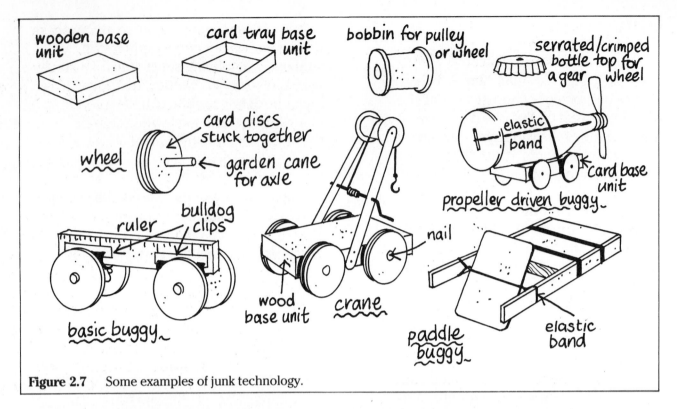

Figure 2.7   Some examples of junk technology.

hack-saw, scissors or snips, and sharp edges can be readily trimmed in a similar fashion or smoothed with a file or sandpaper. Wood, soft plastics and cardboard may be nailed or screwed, but some difficulty may be met when using adhesive on some plastics (see also **Plastics**, page 36).

Junk seems almost ideal for teaching technology, but it does have disadvantages. The first is that, in offering ready-made units, it allows the children to side-step many of the difficult problems that confront them when designing and making. For example, a U-shaped piece used as the uprights and cross-bar of a swing side-steps the difficulty of bridging a gap. The second disadvantage is that of scale. Pieces of junk may have the required shape, but they often do not suit one another in size, and this results in an unattractive and ungainly artefact, unless the collection is made carefully. Relating to scale is a problem which children often have when model making and when solving a problem using junk, children can ignore matters of scale and reality. If a bridge sags a little, then they simply put a convenient tube under the middle. That the tube represents a tower so fat that no ship could squeeze past what is,

in effect, a dam, matters little to the problem-solvers. In other words, junk technology does not lend itself very well to teaching about structures. However, on balance, working with junk is worthwhile provided that its deficiencies are known and are made good by working with other materials.

Paper

When talking about paper here, we refer to the material in its fullest range, from the weakest, semi-transparent, tissue paper to the stoutest, multi-layered cardboard; from the artist's smooth cartridge paper to corrugated, shock-proof, packing paper. Paper is a useful material for teaching technology and, by the nature of things, tends to be readily available in schools.

Teaching technology with paper and card is one way of illustrating the properties of shapes, structures, and simple mechanisms. Flexible and susceptible to shear (tearing), paper reflects some of the properties of materials used in large-scale construction. A large sheet of steel bends and buckles readily unless it is stiffened with corrugations, formed into a tube, or given an L- or H-shaped cross-section. It is the same with

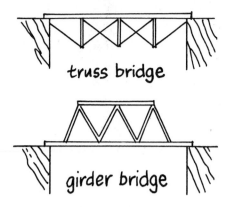

Figure 2.8 Triangular structures in bridges.

paper. A bridge-making problem for juniors to solve with paper may require the use of triangular structures made from paper to stiffen the bridge and tubes to act as supporting pillars. Like steel, paper is springy and can be used as a shock absorber or a spring. An infant might use this property to make a pop-up bee, while a junior might make a weighing device for light objects using a paper spring. Card may also be used to make moving mechanisms which work on the same principles as real machines. Levers may be used in pop-up cards, rotating discs in information cards, and both in a model of a water-wheel.

There are a number of ways of teaching children that strength does not lie only in bulk. One of these is to use paper straws. Although they are inherently weak, they may be used to build strong lattices for such structures as bridges and pylons. Temporary joining can be by means of short lengths of flexible pipe-cleaners, or something similar, which are inserted into the ends of the straws, while PVA makes a more permanent join. Given a pile of straws and an artefact to make, inexperienced children are unlikely to make the elegant structures we might expect. Often, some

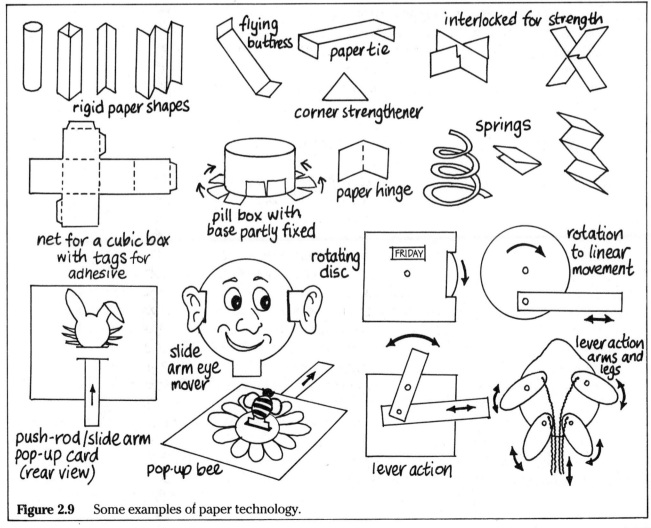

Figure 2.9 Some examples of paper technology.

preparation is needed through, for instance, an examination of the triangles in a bicycle, a bridge, and some scaffolding, together with investigations of the strength of various shapes and structures.

As far as the teacher is concerned, paper is easy to store and easy to manage. Most of its forms may be cut with children's scissors and stuck with PVA or similar adhesive, although the teacher will need to cut stout card to shape. This makes it a very suitable material for introducing the need to consider economic factors. The children can be given a fixed amount of money to spend on their project and must buy their materials from a shop or paper supplier.

At first, it may seem as though paper is the ideal material to teach technology but, like junk, it has its limitations. With a few exceptions, paper and card tend to be used only for making models. Technology is not origami; real artefacts are generally made from more durable materials. Working only with paper also confines children's skill development largely to cutting with scissors and to fixing with adhesive. But, paper, card, scissors and adhesive are readily available and some very useful work can be done with these materials. Paper technology is certainly worthwhile, provided that the children also gain some experience of working with other materials.

Wood

The variety of types of wood equals that of paper. There are *hardwoods* such as oak, beech and ash which are relatively expensive and tend to be difficult to cut and shape with simple tools, and there are *softwoods* such as fir and pine, which are easier to work and often cheaper to buy. The price of wood also depends on its grade. Knotty or cracked wood is usually cheaper, although the knots and cracks can be a nuisance when cutting, drilling, screwing or nailing the wood. However, such low-grade wood is often used in packaging and may be readily available from grocery shops in the high street. It is important to remember that packaging wood is usually undressed; that is, it has not been smoothed and, as a result, there is a danger from wooden splinters.

Some kinds of wood have found particular favour in elementary technology teaching. Balsa, for instance, is a very light and soft wood from Peru and Brazil, once used in making rafts. Its light weight has made it a popular material for model aircraft. Jelutong, from Malaysia, is heavier, shorter-grained, cuts well and drills cleanly, even in small cross-sections. These properties mean that it has become a popular material for teaching about structures. Lengths of this, or a similar wood, can be used to build one, two, and three-dimensional frameworks of some considerable strength. Success often depends on the children's imaginative use of these lightweight frameworks and, in making and using them, they have the opportunity to learn a lot about structural technology. Figure 2.11 shows the fundamentals of this very important and useful approach.

Hardboard is manufactured from processed wood fibre compressed into a

Figure 2.10 Not all paper technology is modelling. This card tag in a ball of wool does not shake free and does not damage the wool.

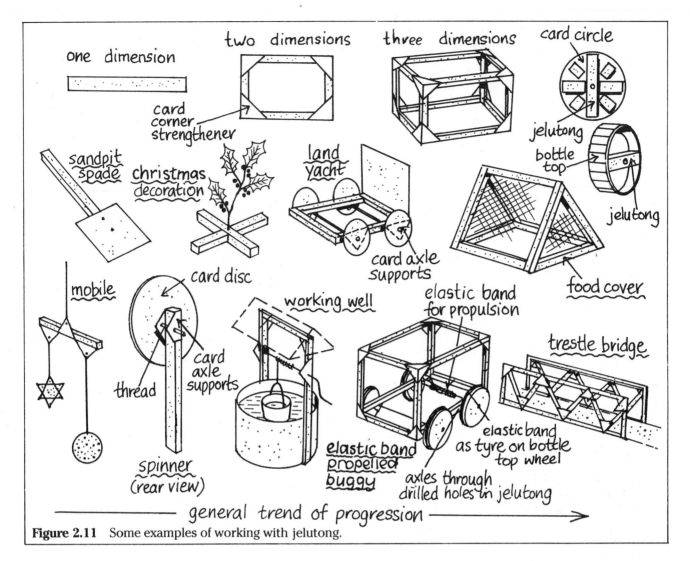

Figure 2.11   Some examples of working with jelutong.

board. Plywood, on the other hand, is made from layers of wood stuck together so that the grain of each layer is at right angles to that of the adjacent layer. This gives it strength and resistance to splitting when being nailed. There are also various blockboards made of strips of wood sandwiched between thinner sheets. Chipboard has wood chips in the sandwich.

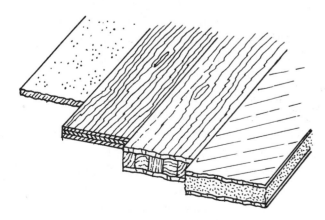

Figure 2.12   A range of boards.

Hardboard and plywood are useful for making panels which only carry a light load, like the sides of a buggy or the baseboard for a dice game. Blockboard and chipboard make strong base-boards and can be used, for instance, as vehicle chassis to which wheels or panels will be attached. Blockboard takes nails better than chipboard.

It is safer for the teacher to cut boards to handy or required sizes where this may present some danger. In any case, children's saws are often too small for the task.

Wood may be cut with a hack-saw, shaped with a file or sanding sticks, smoothed with sandpaper and glasspaper, and drilled using a wheel brace. Fixing can be with PVA, or a similar adhesive, hot-adhesive by a teacher, nails or screws (see also the section on **Tools**, pages 55 to 63). All of these are readily available.

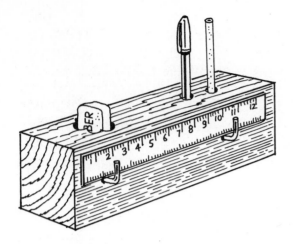

Figure 2.13 A use for a substantial piece of wood as a tidy-bar.

Working in wood extends the children's experience and allows durable, fairly permanent, and often aesthetically pleasing artefacts to be made. Controlling the materials also means that the children's experience can be controlled. Sometimes, it is appropriate to use a substantial piece of timber to solve a problem, as when making a bird table, window box or tidy-bar.

At other times, such pieces would allow design problems to beside-stepped and then one-centimetre square lengths of wood for a structural approach might be provided. It is worthwhile for children to have first-hand experience of technological structures and, although it does not have to be through the medium of small-section wood, this approach has gained some popularity. Wood is more rigid and durable than a paper straw and it is easier to fit wheels and axles, pulleys and cranks, and other simple machines to it. However, faced with a supply of such wood and left to their own devices, inexperienced children are unlikely to produce adequate structures to solve their problems. Some simple exercises to show them the potential of the approach may be needed to put them on the right road, as when making structures with straws as described above. Matchsticks and lollipop sticks may also be used in a structural approach. The former are best used in static artefacts with no moving parts. Lollipop sticks can be cut with snips, but tend to split when drilled, so this limits their usefulness to some degree.

Plastics

Plastics form a complex group of materials whose properties depend on chemical composition and structure. Polyethylterephthalate (PET or terylene) is used for plastic bottles. It can be cut with scissors, snips or a saw but leaves sharp edges. On the other hand, Polypropylene, which is used for kitchenware and syringes, can be cut similarly but leaves softer edges. When repeatedly flexed, PET will eventually snap, whereas polypropylene is resistant to this kind of fracture and so is often used to make boxes with integral lids. Some plastics, such as polypropylene, become softer when heated; others, for example, melamine-formaldehyde, are hardened by heat. There are also others which exist in several forms, each with its own uses. In one form, polystyrene can be hard and brittle and useful for making disposable cups. In another form, it is expanded to make a very light, solid foam used in packaging and for a heat-insulating, wall-covering (Warmaline).

Various kinds of plastics will have been met while working with junk materials and it will be apparent that some are easier to work than others. In general, a stock of the less brittle plastics which cut and drill well will be found useful. Scissors will cut usefully-sized pieces from ice-cream cartons and margarine tubs. Snips may be needed for the thicker, flexible plastics which are used for some kitchen storage boxes. If children need to use plastic bottles or something similar, they may need help in cutting them and they should only use safe scissors or snips *without* points as there is always a danger of cutting tools slipping off curved, smooth surfaces.

One of the properties of plastics which tends to make them useful is that they are usually impermeable to water. They can keep water in, as in a bird bath, or keep water out, as when Corruflute – the plastics equivalent of corrugated card – is used to roof a bird table. Some plastics, being transparent, are useful as substitutes for glass as when half of a bottle or plastic film is used as a propagator cover. As well as making artefacts completely in plastics, children may use plastics in conjunction with other materials. Flexible plastics, for instance, may be used to make hinges.

While plastics are often easily fixed to other materials with screws and nails, they can be difficult to join together themselves. PVA will stick some plastics, but it is not waterproof; a latex adhesive (like Copydex) may work with fabric-like materials, but hot adhesive will melt many plastics. Often the solution is to pop-rivet the pieces together (see **Tools**, page 61).

(**NB** Never let children use non-approved adhesives or attempt to melt plastics together as the fumes can be dangerous.)

On occasions, plastics are the most appropriate material for the task in hand. A stock of plastics in block and sheet form should be available for those occasions. Plastic straws may be used in a structural approach as an alternative to paper straws. They are available in several diameters and some have a corrugated, flexible section. Flexible plastic tubing is also useful.

Figure 2.14   Some examples of artefacts made from plastics. Note that washers and axle supports may also be made from this material.

Metals

Of all the metals, one in particular lends itself well to working with simple tools and that is aluminium. Once so rare that Napoleon was flattered with a gift of aluminium cutlery, this light, silvery-white metal is now everywhere: as cooking-foil around food, 'silver' paper on sweets, milk bottle tops, confectionery cases, drink

cans, pans, window frames, car-engine parts, lorry and coach panels, and many other places where its light weight and resistance to corrosion are important.

At its thinnest, it is easily torn or cut with scissors. Thicker material may be drilled, sawn and filed much like wood. However, unlike wood, it can be shaped, bent, twisted or flattened with a hammer, if necessary holding it with a vice or clamp. Sharp or rough edges are easily filed smooth, and corners may be bent over and nipped with pliers. Pieces of aluminium can be fixed together with small bolts or pop-riveted (see **Tools**, page 61). Where the pieces are not under tension, PVA or hot adhesive, perhaps applied by the teacher, will make an adequate join.

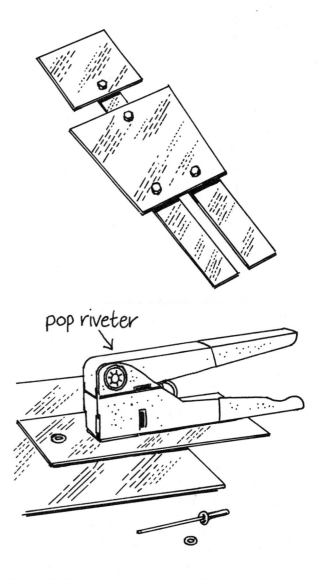

pop riveter

Figure 2.15   Bolting and pop riveting aluminium.

The forms in which aluminium is generally available to the teacher lend themselves to a teaching progression. Young children may be introduced to the thinner aluminium foils, shaping them with scissors and by hand, moulding them around objects, and fixing them in place with PVA or drawing pins. They might use it to make a model robot or a boat, for example. Older children may saw, drill, bend and rivet thicker pieces of the metal. The safety precautions needed when working aluminium are similar to those for working wood, with the possible addition of gloves if sharp or ragged pieces are being produced. A whole artefact might be made in aluminium or only a piece for an artefact. Being a metal, aluminium is a good conductor of electricity and so may be used to make simple switches in, for instance, burglar alarm circuits.

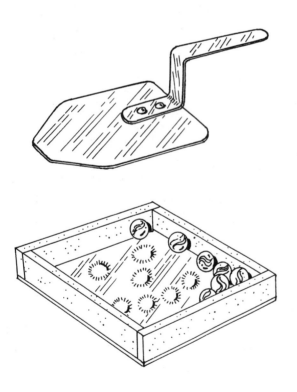

Figure 2.16 A trowel and a game made from thin aluminium sheet.

Aluminium foil is obtainable in quantity from the kitchen. Small, thin sheets can be cut from cans by the teacher and trimmed to remove ragged edges. Many cans made

38

of steel and coated with tin (and thus called *tins*) are unsuitable. They may be distinguished from aluminium cans by their bottoms. The steel can has a bottom attached by a rim to match the top. In the aluminium can, the bottom and the sides are moulded as one, smooth unit. If in doubt, a magnet will pick out the steel cans. Slightly thicker and very useful off-cuts of sheet aluminium may also be obtained as waste from garages that undertake body repairs.

Fabrics

One of the traditional craft materials is fabric. The Code of 1880, an earlier National Curriculum, required that girls be taught 'plain needlework', but working with fabrics in a wide variety of ways is not unusual for younger boys and girls in such areas as art and craft. In technology, however, it is *not* 'plain needlework'. Working with fabrics offers the same opportunities for creative design and realisation as other materials, whether a child is using fabrics in a Nativity display at Christmas, or in making a puppet or a craft apron.

For younger children a collection of binca, cotton, felt, gingham, and fabric scraps, like simulated fur, are useful. The usual school scissors should suffice for cutting materials which may then be joined using PVA. Buttons, useful for eyes, may be attached with thread.

Children who are a little older may be introduced to tapes and trimmings like rickrack braid and lace trimming. These are useful embellishments for artefacts such as a pencil case or table mat. Wools, yarns and embroidery threads make other things possible. For example, each child might design, make and contribute a simple piece for a 'Bayeux-type' tapestry. With kapok, or old nylon tights, stuffed toys and block-printed cushions are possible. Permanent joining can be made by means of a needle and thread or PVA, as appropriate. Temporary joining could be with buttons, a nylon tape fastener like Velcro, press studs, or hook and eye fasteners.

This fabric collection can be extended for older children to include gauze, buttercloth or nylon net to make an airy, flyproof food cover, unbleached cotton for designing and making a craft apron, and surplus wool for a co-operative effort in knitted rug making, where each child contributes a square to the agreed design. Permanent joining would be by any appropriate method and a 'rapid hemmer' could be a useful tool here. Temporary joining might include a zip for the more adept.

The tools appropriate here are fairly self-evident: safe scissors, needles, needle threaders, pins, knitting needles, tape measure, thimbles, and possibly a rapid hemmer.

Figure 2.17   Some examples of fabric technology.

Food

Everyone thinks they know about working with food for, after all, we eat it every day. It is also another of the traditional craft areas and this, of course, has its dangers because established practices and past experiences tend to predispose teachers towards particular ways of working with the material. The focus of food technology is not the recipe but the problem to be solved, the need to be fulfilled, or the opportunity to be taken. Food should be seen as another material, like paper, wood, plastics, metals and fabrics. Just as with other materials, food needs to be prepared, shaped, or processed to make an artefact. The artefact might be a sugar mouse designed and made by an infant, or a salad created by an older child.

The tools used in food technology would range from a round-ended, blunt knife and spoon for cutting, shaping and peeling by infants as they make sweetmeats, cress sandwiches (having first grown their own cress), and jellies. A whisk could be introduced for making cold desserts with the opportunity to examine its mechanisms and see the changes which can occur in materials. Older children could use the apple corer and a fork in making baked apples and potatoes (with appropriate consideration of safety made by the teacher).

Juniors could begin to combine these items to make a meal. They could design and make a packed lunch and toasted sandwiches (under supervision). They might also respond to a need, perhaps a school fair, by making pies, tarts, biscuits and bread buns, costing them and pricing them realistically. This would require safe forms of common cooking and baking utensils. An oven, microwave or otherwise, extends the range of feasible activities. Some of the examples given in the National Curriculum do assume that one is available, but the teacher must have firm rules about its use and always plan for the safety of the children, ensuring that ovens are clean and checked regularly.

While it is relatively easy to provide a making activity which children can do, it is also easy to let it slip away from the aims of technology education. Perceiving a need and designing can become, 'What shall we do today? Where's the recipe book?' and food technology degenerates into cookery.

Setting the task in a context or sketching a scenario can help to avoid this. For example:

Our Christmas Party is only two weeks away. Let's plan the party. We have only £x to spend and we need some food, something to drink, and some presents and games. If we make as much as possible ourselves, it would save a lot of money.

Groups of children can then work on different aspects of the problem; some design and make games, some work on gifts, others organise and make food, drink, and prepare a party room.

Other materials

There are a number of alternative materials which are well-suited to a particular kind of task. One of these is spaghetti. The rigid, uncooked rods may be used instead of straws in teaching about structures.

Concrete and plaster of Paris are materials specifically mentioned in the National Curriculum documents. Unlike most of the materials described above, their properties change considerably when processed. Concrete may be bought ready-bagged in a dry form requiring only the addition of water. Only small quantities should be kept in stock since, once opened, its shelf life is limited. It may be used for making outdoor ornaments or plant pots by casting in plastic containers. The finished artefact can be removed in about 24 hours or so. Pupils in a school in Dyfed made and painted life-size concrete puffins to attract the birds back to Cardigan Island. Plaster of Paris may be used similarly for indoor artefacts. Modelling clay, especially that which does not need firing, is also a useful extension to the range of materials.

There is no limit to the materials which technology may draw on and, for the classroom, the imaginative teacher will be able to extend this list. In using any material, however, what needs to be considered is safety and whether the material can be shaped, cut, and joined with what is available in the classroom.

40

Kits

Although kits are not, strictly speaking, a material, it is appropriate to comment on their use here since, in many ways, they are treated much like a recyclable material.

There are various kinds of construction sets for realising designs. They tend to differ in three main ways:
• their material;
• their method of joining;
• their capacity.

Each of these needs to be considered when selecting a technology kit.

The most common materials are wood, plastics and metal. Wood tends to be used for solid building blocks, plastics for tubes and strips, and metal for strips. The method of joining is determined largely by the material (and whether someone else has already patented it). Wooden blocks, for instance, may be stacked loosely, plastic tubes may have snap-on fasteners, while perforated plastic and metal strips may use nuts and bolts. The capacity of a kit has two aspects, its versatility and its potential for making sophisticated artefacts. For versatility, it should be possible to make a wide variety of artefacts with the kit, beyond those which may be described by the manufacturer. Kits which can be made into only one or two artefacts, usually following a set of step-by-step instructions, do not have a great deal to offer in solving open-ended problems. Ideally, a kit should lend itself to making any appropriate artefact that a child designs. In practice, no such kit exists but some are definitely more versatile than others. Since the size of a kit is limited by cost, versatility is achieved with components which can be used in many ways. Wooden blocks make a more versatile construction kit than the same number of specially shaped pieces which lock together to make only a toy car. However, the toy car might use levers, cogs and gears not available to the loose-block constructor. To the extent that the toy car illustrates a higher level of technological capability, it is more sophisticated than a pile of blocks. Additional sophistication may be achieved with more specialised components. A kit which is to be versatile *and* sophisticated tends to have many multi-purpose units, like strips and tubes, and a number of more specialised units not easily manufactured from the others, like wheels, axles, cogs and gears. Such kits exist and are used by technologists to test ideas before proceeding to more expensive stages. In a classroom, a kit should be versatile and sophisticated enough to solve problems appropriate to the age and ability of the children giving due regard to their manipulative skills. This makes it possible to tailor kits to the needs of particular age ranges.

For younger children, there are shaped, wooden building blocks which stack loosely or are joined by a tongue and groove method. The shapes often include solid triangles, arches and cylinders, as well as rectangular blocks and lend themselves well to making static artefacts, like houses, bridges, garages and shops. Some of these blocks are brick-sized and made of card or plastic. **Sticklebricks** are plastic blocks of various shapes which are covered in spines. They are joined by pressing them together so that the spines interlock.

Artefacts made with these can differ in kind to those of free-standing, wooden blocks because they do not fall apart so easily. **Mobilo** is a kit of plastic, interlocking, skeleton squares and cubes which will make large, static artefacts. **Big Builder** consists of large, perforated plastic strips which are fixed together with plastic nuts and bolts. Some versions use wooden, perforated strips. The artefacts these make are large and may be made mobile with the kit's wheels. **Constructor** is similar but also includes interlocking blocks and some gear wheels. **Quadro** is a kit of plastic tubes which clip together to make child-sized artefacts. **Duplo** uses a large-scale version of the well-known **LEGO** blocks which snap together to make large artefacts. Some of the **Quadro** kits include a 'mini design kit' for developing ideas and designs before constructing a large scale version, a useful practice to encourage.

Many of these kits will still be useful with older children, who might also use **Meccano**, a kit of strips which use nuts and bolts for joining. Versions made of wood, plastic, or metal units, are available, the last usually being intended for older children.

The basic unit of the extensive range of **LEGO** kits is a small plastic block, joined to others by pressing the pieces together. There are kits to suit any age and ability, including materials for illustrating computer control. **Clixi** is a kit of plastic, flat shapes and rods which are joined by a bead and socket method. Among other things, it may be used to illustrate cog and gear mechanisms. **Plawcotech** is a system of rods with push-fit connectors and will illustrate a range of mechanisms and computer control. **Capsela** uses waterproof capsules which snap together and can be used to make motorised land and water vehicles, which also may be controlled by a computer. A number of kits will illustrate computer control, but the hardware and software needed to make this possible may have to be bought from a separate source.

Kits use different materials, different units, and different methods of joining. Ultimately, these are what limit a kit's versatility but may also make it well-suited to a particular group of children. Those with little manipulative skill may be frustrated by fiddly fasteners, and so jumbo-sized pieces which make structures quickly might be more satisfactory. On the other hand, more adept and experienced children might be equally frustrated with a kit which lacks the capacity for realising more sophisticated designs.

A kit removes the need to work materials as there is no sawing, cutting, drilling, smoothing or painting to do. It also takes away the need to choose materials and suit actions to them. At the same time, the units of a kit and its method of joining often design out the very problem we want the children to solve. Most kits may be used to build a bridge, for instance, but the child learns little about the technological problems of bridging a gap because the kit's pieces are designed to stay together, come what may. On the other hand, the kit makes success independent of a child's ability to work materials. Removing this skills barrier can increase the likelihood of a successful artefact being produced. It also opens a door to more sophisticated technology with, for instance, mechanisms and computer control.

Many kits come with step-by-step instructions for making models. Although the ultimate goal of technology teaching is not to teach children to follow recipe cards, these can be useful. Children's experiences differ so greatly that some will need more time than others to learn how to use the components and find out what they can do. 'Recipe' cards are useful for providing that experience in a structured way. These can be supplemented by activities which open the task a little. For instance, if a child has made a fixed crane by following the instructions, then the teacher could ask how it might be made to turn on its base, using components in the kit. The aim is to reach the stage where the child makes an artefact which is not described in the instruction book.

Chapter three

Information technology

'Information Technology is concerned with storing, processing and presenting information by electronic means' *(Information Technology Capability; Non-Statutory Guidance, A1).*

For any active, living thing, the most valuable commodity of all is information. Without it, purposeful activity is impossible. For most of our existence, the brain has stored, processed and presented information. Sometimes this process has been easy, but often it has been laborious, slow and fallible. Writing reduced the burden of information storage and the abacus helped in some simple processing tasks, yet the invention of mechanical calculating machines, like 19-year-old Blaise

Pascal's cogwheel adding machine, made little impact. They were expensive and, given the ease with which the abacus could be used to the same effect, perhaps redundant technology. However, in 1834 Charles Babbage made a significant advance with his design for an analytical engine. This was nothing less than a mechanical computer which was fed instructions and data on punched cards, like the automatic looms of the time. The instructions and data were stored in the machine and there was to be a means of displaying the outcome of its deliberations. In spite of Babbage's enormous efforts, a working engine was never completed because its components were beyond the technological capabilities of the time.

One of the main sources of vast quantities of unprocessed information in the second half of the nineteenth century was the census return. Sorted and collated by hand, processing was slow and laborious. In the USA, Herman Hollerith had the data of the 1890 census returns recorded on punched cards and read rapidly by machines designed to detect electrically the presence of the holes.

One of the first computers to do more than sorting tasks was Colossus, built in 1943 during the Second World War to break German codes. Like the radios of the time, it used electronic valves in glass envelopes. Colossus was a successful code breaker but was not a general purpose computer. ENIAC, built in Pennsylvania in 1945, had some 18,000 valves and is generally regarded as the first, true, electronic computer. Computers like this were large, took a lot of power, used fragile valves and could not be programmed from a keyboard. Programming was done by plugging in lots of wire leads.

The invention of the transistor in 1947–8, the integrated circuit in 1958 and their subsequent miniaturisation in succeeding decades made it possible for computers to shrink from Goliaths to the book size they are today. Hand-held electronic calculators made their debut in the early 1970s. The impact of the microchip on information storage and processing is so enormous that information technology is taken to imply that an electronic means is involved, hence its inclusion in the description of information technology quoted at the beginning of the chapter.

The role of information technology

There is hardly an area of information handling in which information technology does not seem to have a potential application. Opportunities to use it have been taken in an enormous range of activities. In banking, for instance, it is used to process accounts, to transfer information from place to place and to offer different services through electronic machines operated by 'smart' cards. Similarly, businesses rely on computers to manage payrolls and stock. The bar code reading device at the supermarket checkout is one of the store computer's data collectors for monitoring sales and stock. The computer processes the data, prepares accounts and re-orders goods. Information services like Ceefax are up-dated minute by minute. Diagnoses in hospitals are aided by information

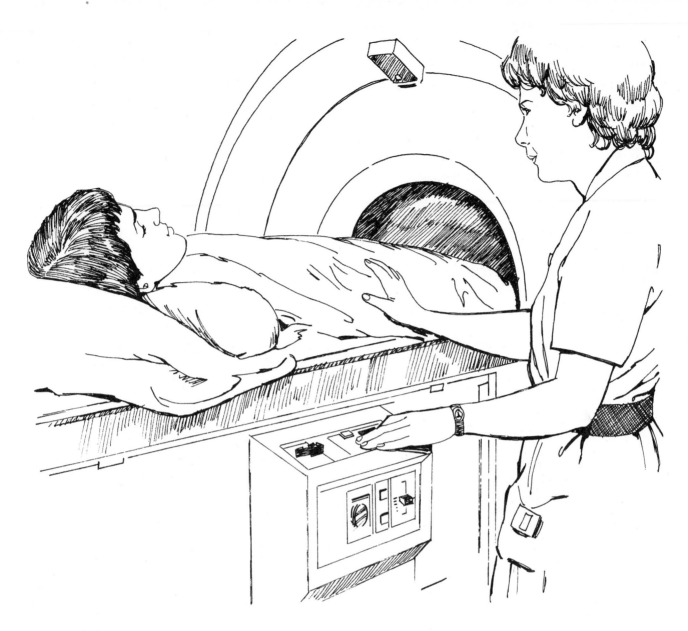

technology. Body scanners, for instance, collect information about the internal organs which is then computer-processed to produce a meaningful picture for the surgeon. Computers can monitor the information fed back from various sensors fitted to a car and maximise the efficiency of its engine, plan the best route to take, and warn of hazards or malfunctions. Even the weather is monitored by computers, while aircraft pilots train in flight simulators and children learn with the help of a computer.

In the home, there are many devices which collect and process information, and then act on the outcome. The video-recorder responds to the user's instructions either supplied through a keyboard or from a remote control device.

Music systems and electronic keyboards use the microchip, and washing machines, ovens and even children's toys often have similar components.

As far as technology is concerned, electronics can solve many problems. For example, a motion sensor may pick up movement in a house and pass on the information to trigger an alarm. Inevitably, there will be false alarms, perhaps caused by a moving curtain or a falling petal from a vase of flowers. Similarly, a heat sensor might give false alarms because of the presence of radiators. However, if the two are put together and their information is fed to a processor which notes when one sensor *and* the other sensor have both detected something before it switches on the alarm, the problem is solved or, at least

Data from market research is stored and processed to identify and clarify opportunities for applying technology. In design, computers assist the technologist to explore and develop ideas and present them in forms ranging from the presentation material used to discuss and appraise the potential of an idea to the technical drawings for turning it into reality. Often, prototype production is expensive so as much as possible of the work is done by computer. It presents the artefact from all its viewpoints, simulates its operation, tests the effect of modifications, and prepares plans which minimise waste. At the making stage, the machines which manufacture the components may be guided and instructed by computer. This is known as computer-aided-manufacture (CAM). Sometimes, this means the control of a machine like a lathe for shaping wood or metal, at other times, it is the control of a robot whose arm lifts, places, turns, loads, unloads, drills, welds or sprays the artefact. Few artefacts reach the market today without some form of packaging, logo or instructions and the computer may again play a part in their design and production. Each of these uses of information technology in technology is itself the satisfaction of a need or solution to a problem.

Information technology education

The role of information technology in industry, commerce and our daily lives is so great that its place in the curriculum seems self-evident. However, utility is not the sole justification for its inclusion. After all, there is much that is useful which does not have a place in every child's education. Reading and writing open doors to a wider, richer world. What can information technology capability offer?

• Information technology is a legitimate part of technology, both as a tool used to facilitate the processes of technology, and

the margin for error is reduced to an acceptable level. In a large office block, the state of the environment might be sampled by sensors of light, temperature and humidity which pass the information on to a central computer. This in turn, operates the lighting, heating and humidity controls, taking into account weekends and holidays. The ability of the microchip to take decisions and act on them allows the technologist to use them for the automatic control of machines, systems and environments.

Not only does technology use the microchip to solve problems, but it also uses it in the processes of problem solving.

as product of technology, generated in the attempt to solve a problem or satisfy a need. As such, the justification for its presence rests ultimately on the case for technology education.

• Information technology capability has the potential to be useful in acquiring knowledge and understanding in other areas of the curriculum and, after school, it may enhance the competence of the individual in many facets of life – in leisure, at home and at work.

• In developing information technology capability, it may promote logical and precise thinking, and information-finding skills applicable in other areas of the curriculum and in life generally.

• There is the need to develop a critical awareness of the role of information technology in all the facets of our lives. It is important to know its strengths and weakness, its advantages and disadvantages and that it can be fallible.

Information technology is not delivered solely by technology; other areas of the curriculum will contribute to the development of information technology capability. However, the unique contribution of technology education is likely to be in the first area listed, but the work will almost inevitably make contributions in other areas. The National Curriculum emphasises five strands of information technology capability to be

cultivated: developing ideas and communicating information, handling information, modelling, measurement and control, and applications and effects. The first three are to do with using information technology as a tool, the fourth is about using it to solve technological problems, and the last considers its broader aspects.

Developing ideas and communicating information

The computer organises and presents text in forms that are different to those the children are able to produce by hand. Similarly, illustrations can often be integrated with the text, taken from a bank of pictures stored in the software or drawn on the screen with the help of that software; even sound effects can be included. The aim is to work with this facility just as we would with pencil and paper, to think with the medium and sketch ideas, abandoning some and developing others. It is not meant to be merely a device for transcribing written work so that it might be presented in a neater form. It is an alternative to pencil and paper with its own advantages and disadvantages. In technology, this use relates directly to generating a design proposal and to planning. Specialist 'technology' programmes are not necessary. Very young children may need the help of an emanuensis – someone to type in the information – or an overlay keyboard to use the computer in this way. Older children might learn to set aside a computer page as a memo board to store ideas and reminders until needed.

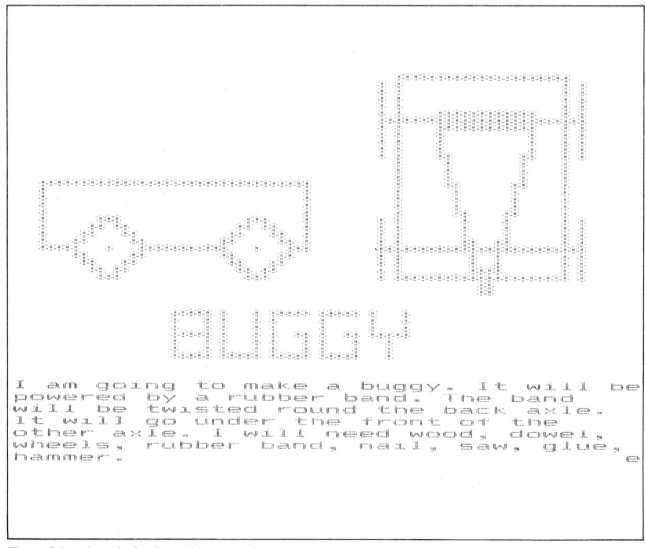

Figure 3.1   A work plan for making a simple buggy.

48

In using the word processing capability to plan the sequence of actions which will be followed in the making stage, children might produce a work sequence sheet like that below. The tasks are ticked off on completion. Where children are working in groups, it could also show who will do each task.

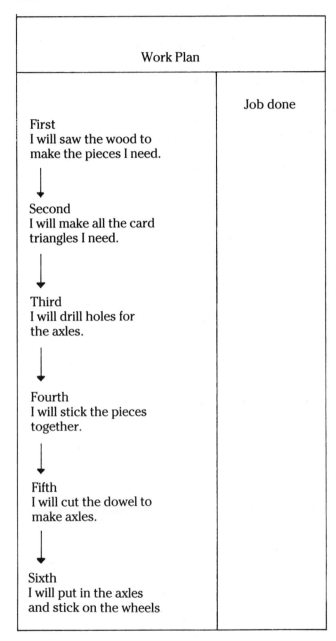

Work Plan	
	Job done
First I will saw the wood to make the pieces I need. ↓ Second I will make all the card triangles I need. ↓ Third I will drill holes for the axles. ↓ Fourth I will stick the pieces together. ↓ Fifth I will cut the dowel to make axles. ↓ Sixth I will put in the axles and stick on the wheels.	

Handling information

The computer is particularly adept at storing and sorting large quantities of information. When children do a survey and collect a lot of data, the advantages of this facility will be immediate and apparent to the child. At its simplest, the procedure might be to use a suitable word-processing package and create organised lists. For example, before making a bird table, children might survey the range of birds which come to collect crumbs on the school yard with the intention of suiting the size of the bird table to the birds. Their data might be entered in the form:

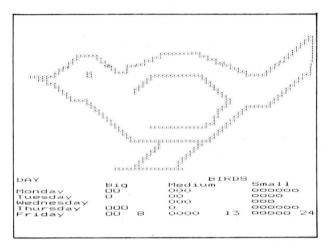

Figure 3.2   Data for bird visitors.

This would be saved and later retrieved for the addition of more data on subsequent occasions. Older children might use software which identifies their birds and tells them their sizes so that they can be entered into a simple database. Later, the results would be automatically collated and presented as charts and graphs.

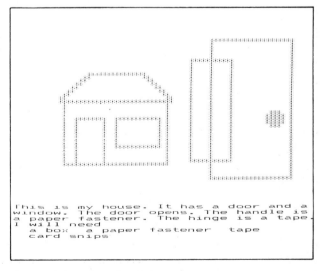

Figure 3.3   An infant's house.

Modelling

Modelling, or simulating events, systems, or processes is an important role for the computer. Initially, children can see that it has this capacity through adventure games and through software like *HONEYPOT*, a package for primary technology which sets its activities in the context of an imaginary village and its valley. It provides opportunities for discussion, designing and making in response to problems as they arise in the course of events. Some programs model real systems and environments, like the working of a water-mill, for instance, or the heating of a house. These might be used to point to the need for automatic devices for controlling the mill and stabilising the temperature of a house.

Measurement and control

A key function of information technology is to provide automatic measurement and control. The first step is to make children aware of its existence in the familiar world around them, for example, in the microwave cooker, the automatic washer, the video-recorder, the central heating system and, of course, their own toys. Bigtrak, Roamer, PIP and other programmable toys are useful for giving children direct experience of bringing about a complex chain of actions according to their instructions. The computer-directed turtle extends this work. Simple, programmable robots take it a stage further.

These 'packages' are ready-made examples of control technology, but it is possible to use simple computer control in the children's own designing and making activities. To complete a model lighthouse, for instance, the light might be set to flash according to a simple program provided by the pupil. A buggy's motor could be controlled similarly. At a more sophisticated level, a set of traffic lights might be programmed to simulate real traffic lights. Kits of hardware, its associated software, and instructions are

available from information technology suppliers. Sometimes, these are made in forms suited to particular age ranges so there is the need to ensure that the correct one is selected.

While the previous examples use the computer to process the information, many forms of control do not. They require instead a unit to sense or detect a change (the information), another unit to process that information and pass on the outcome of its deliberations (the processor), and a final unit which acts upon information received (the output). This is shown schematically in Figure 3.4.

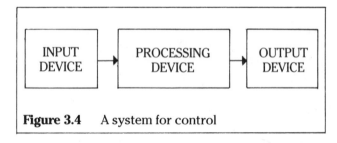

Figure 3.4   A system for control

For example, if a light is to be switched on automatically when it becomes dark, the *input* is handled by a light detector, the *processor* monitors what the light detector finds and, when the level of light falls below a certain level, it triggers the *output* device to switch on the light. These units are in boxes designed to plug into one another and are available with a range of functions; for example, one will detect light, another will detect temperature and a different one will pick up sound.

Applications and effects

This strand is aimed at widening the children's awareness of the uses and role of technology in the real world. To begin with, the uses of information technology in the children's direct experience would provide the source material; the purpose of bar codes, for example, and the strips on the plastic cards used in cash dispensers and telephones. This would lead to comparisons between the different ways of doing things, with and without information technology. What happens in shops and libraries that do not use the bar codes? What do we have to do when there is no cardphone? Does information technology make it easier, more efficient or better? What happens when things go wrong? As well as pointing to the possible inconvenience and even dangers inherent in a dependence on information technology hardware, this also leads to the accuracy of what it has to say and that any piece of software is only as good as those who write it, give it information, and subsequently use it.

Choosing software

Choosing software is, in some ways, no different from choosing a good textbook. We want it to communicate successfully, to use effective teaching strategies and to be an interesting and worthwhile alternative to other ways of working. At the same time, there are important differences between a piece of software and a book. For example, a book is deaf to the response of the reader while a piece of software can enter into some form of dialogue with its user. On the other hand, as one of the oldest pieces of educational technology, the book needs no instruction manual or box of electronics and tolerates some physical abuse. The enormous difference between the book and the computer tends to conceal what is often a common purpose, that is, effective teaching and learning. To begin with, it can be useful to forget this physical difference and judge a piece of software as you would

a textbook. Is the language pitched at the appropriate level? Are the illustrations likely to be effective? What kind of learning does it support – rote, understanding, or higher levels? However, the differences cannot be ignored altogether. If a child opens a book at the wrong page, the book does not lock itself shut. Compare this with what happens with some software if the wrong key is pressed.

The appraisal of a piece of software cannot, of course, be divorced from its purpose. To do so would be like condemning a dictionary because its plot is weak! Computers can play a number of roles in the classroom. They can, for example, be used like a teacher and demonstrate, instruct, exercise and simulate aspects of the topic being studied. On the other hand, they can be used as a store and processor of information, like a 'super-calculator'. Verbal and non-verbal information might be placed in a datafile or spreadsheet by a child or the computer might collect it through external probes, as in some science activities. Often, the computer also does calculations with the

information and reports the outcome to the user. Sometimes, the information is used to control some device outside the computer; a heater might be switched off when the temperature reaches some predetermined level, for example. The computer can also be used to present information. It might be used as a typewriter or to present information in tables or graphs or to draw plans or diagrams of artefacts.

While there are pieces of software which serve one of these functions only, in practice, it is not uncommon to find that there is some overlap. A program which collects and processes data may also present a copy as a table, graph or pie chart. The National Curriculum requires that children acquire some facility in using information technology to store, process and present information and to appreciate the computer's potential and modelling control, but the use of the computer as a surrogate teacher is a matter for the teacher. It is important, therefore, that these functions are not confused. Using the computer only as a surrogate teacher is unlikely to meet the requirements of the National Curriculum.

To make the process of evaluating software clearer, an evaluation schedule is provided on page 53 (developed from an earlier version, first published in the MUSE magazine, *Information Technology and Learning*, 13(2), pp. 83–86). Applied to software which a school already has, the schedule will at least help to identify areas of strength and weakness so that some remedial action, supplementary teaching or other support can be planned. After a little practice, the schedule may be replaced by an informal process relying on the educated critical sense. The first step is to determine the function of any software offered. If this does not match the needs then it is pointless to proceed. Equally, there are some general criteria which should usually be met, and after that there will be specific questions relating to how well the material fulfils its function or functions. After the first block of questions, it is only necessary to consider those sections relating to the role that the program is intended to have in the classroom. The answer 'yes' to most of the *relevant* questions indicates a software package worth trying out on children.

Software evaluation schedule

Some general considerations
- Is the cost acceptable for the package?
- Do you find the teacher's notes adequate for your needs?
- Can the package be used with little or no teacher support as the children use it, that is:
  - is the verbal information likely to be effective with those who will use it/is it readable/does it avoid computer jargon?
  - are the illustrations/graphics likely to be effective with those who will use it?
  - can a pupil press a wrong key without things going wrong?
- Does the software avoid effects which may disturb others (eg noises – it may be possible to switch them off)?
- Other

If the answer to some or all of these questions is NO, is it worth proceeding?

Some considerations regarding the role of teacher
- Does the instruction fit in with or extend appropriately your scheme of work, ie is it relevant?
- As far as you can judge, is the information accurate, free from unwanted bias, and sufficiently up to date?
- For the kind of learning you require (rote, understanding, application, problem solving etc), does the program provide it?
- Is the material likely to achieve the required learning at least as efficiently as other means at your disposal?
- Will those who use it find the activity interesting/ motivating?
- Does the software provide opportunities for worthwhile, active participation?
- Does the software provide feedback for the user?
- Could the package be profitably used with children of a relatively wide range of ability?
- Does the software keep records of pupil interaction for teacher inspection?
- Other

Some considerations regarding the role of information presenter
- Will the pupil be able to cope with the organising commands, menus, etc or is help available, if appropriate?

- Will the pupil be able to print a copy of the information unaided or is help available, if appropriate?
- Is what you see on the screen very similar to what you get when a copy is made?
- Does the software have the facility to save the information for editing at a later date?
- Other

Some considerations regarding the role of information handler
- Is the package relevant to the needs of the scheme of work or pupil?
- From the point of view of the pupil, does the software process the information in more than a trivial way?
- If incorrect information is fed in, does the program allow it to be corrected?
- Does the package keeps records of pupil interaction?
- Does the package allow copies of the pupil's work to be made?
- Other

Some considerations regarding the role of modeller
- Is the situation modelled meaningful/relevant to the pupil?
- Will the pupil be able to cope with the commands and menus which control the model or simulation, or is someone available to help, if appropriate?
- If an error is made in entering a command, does the software prompt or allow correction?
- Other

Some considerations regarding the role of measurer and controller
- Is the kind of control suited to the ability of the child?
- Do the control commands or does the programming language have meaning for the child?
- Is the hardware robust enough?
- Is the hardware safe to use?
- Will the pupil be able to use the hardware readily?
- Will the interface allow damage to the computer if a faulty connection or command occurs?
- Other

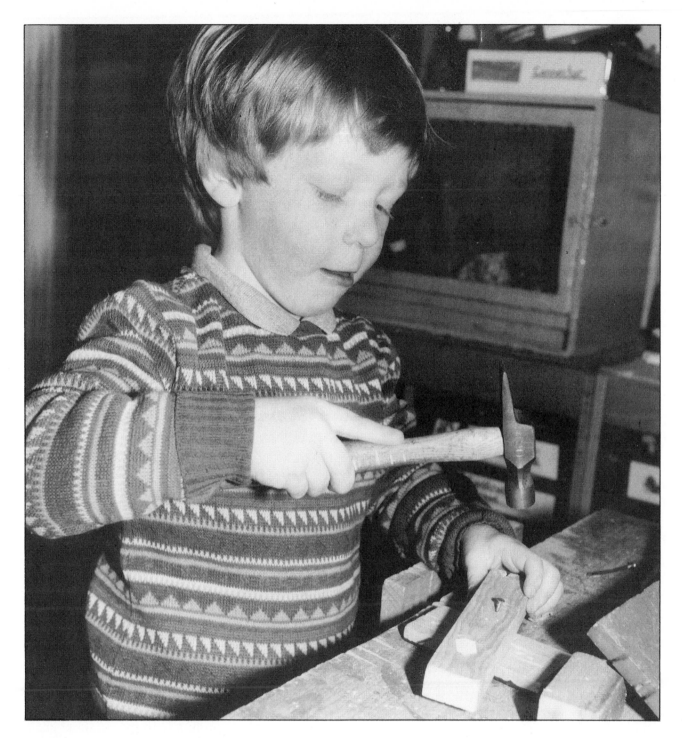

Chapter four

Tools and working skills

Tools have functions which tend to fall into a small number of categories such as holding, cutting, shaping, drilling, joining, and finishing. Each tool is designed for a specific task. If great force is needed in using one, then it may be the wrong tool for the job or the right tool but used incorrectly. Whatever the reason, great force is to be avoided because it often leads to accidents through loss of control of the tool and the material. It is important, therefore, that children learn to select and use tools correctly.

Holding

In order to work materials properly, they need to be held firmly. There are a number of ways of doing this.

The bench hook

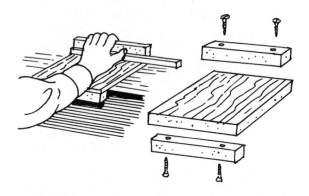

Figure 4.1 Bench hook in use and its components.

This is a simple sawing aid which hooks over the edge of a table or bench. The material which is to be sawn is pressed firmly to the back of the hook by the heel of the hand, an action which also secures the hook against the edge of the table. The material to be sawn should then project to the right or left according to whether the child is right- or left-handed.

Bench hooks are easy to make and all that is needed are three pieces of wood and four screws.

The vice

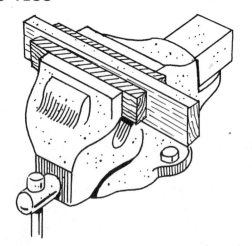

Figure 4.2 The use of scraps of wood to protect materials in the jaws of a vice.

56

Vices hold materials more firmly than they can be held on a bench hook and also leave both hands free. They are available in a variety of sizes, although very heavy ones need to be bolted or screwed to a bench. Lighter vices, suitable for children, usually have an integral clamp on the underside so that they can be fixed to a bench simply by turning a short toggle bar. If necessary, such vices can be removed from the bench when not in use.

Vices, of course, are capable of exerting very large forces and can crush some materials. When it is important that the jaws do not mark the material, it should be sandwiched between pieces of card or scrap wood.

The clamp

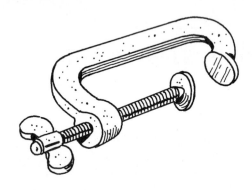

Figure 4.3 A G-clamp or cramp.

There is a very wide range of clamps (or cramps) available. However, some are very specialised and not likely to be of general use in the classroom. Various kinds of G-clamp, on the other hand, can be useful, especially when dealing with materials of an awkward shape or size which the vice cannot grip.

Pliers

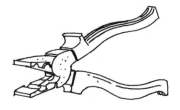

Figure 4.4 Pliers.

Pliers are really a combination of tools and can be used for holding, gripping and cutting. The serrated nose of the pliers is for holding flat materials, while the circular section behind the nose is for gripping curved surfaces like wooden dowel and metal tube. Children may find pliers particularly useful for holding nails in place when hammering, rather than using their fingers.

Behind the gripping areas of the pliers there is usually a section for snipping wire or other thin pieces of metal. With some pliers, thin wire may also be snipped in the slots on the back of the hinge.

Even those who are adept at using scissors occasionally nip themselves with pliers. The cardinal rule with all tools is not to exert any pressure until the fingers are out of the way; a habit worth developing at an early age.

Cutting, shaping and drilling

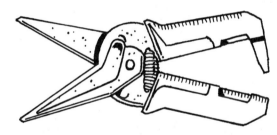

Figure 4.5   Snips.

The purpose of cutting, shaping and drilling is, in essence, to remove unwanted material. The most common cutting tools used in schools are scissors and children learn to use them in many areas of the curriculum. Scissor-like snips are useful for cutting thicker card. They are used in the same way as scissors and therefore need no further description.

Teachers themselves will find craft knives useful for cutting and preparing card and plastics but, of course, they are dangerous items if left lying around and in the wrong hands.

Other cutting tools include pliers, which have already been described, and saws.

The hack-saw

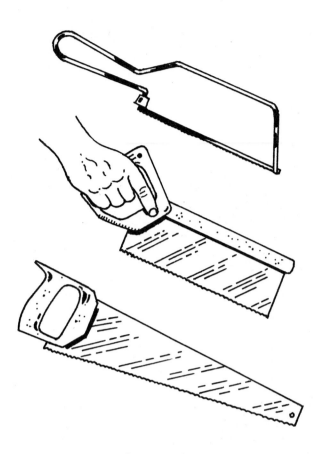

Figure 4.6   A variety of saws.

The hack-saw is available in long- and short-blade forms. The short-blade one, known as the junior hack-saw, is so-called because of its size and not because it was designed for juniors. However, it is very suitable for young children and will cut wood or metal. Its teeth point away from the handle so that it cuts when pushed forwards.

Beginners often have difficulty in using a saw smoothly so that it does not jam in the cut. The usual cause of this seems to be a reluctance to let the saw do the job; in short, too much force is used. If children hold the saw loosely, moving it backwards and forwards without significant downward pressure, a smooth cutting action will be developed. Cuts should be started by a few backward pulls on the saw.

Children often have a tendency to use only a part of the saw blade, possibly through a fear of it jamming. It is more efficient to use the full length of the blade and a cleaner cut will result.

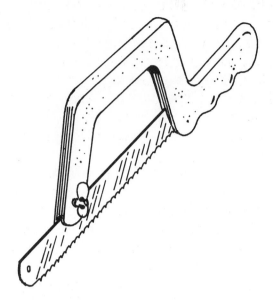

Figure 4.7   Knife-style hack-saw.

Longer hack-saws are often difficult for children to manage safely, but one kind uses long blades in a knife-like handle and is used much like a knife which cuts when pushed forwards. This is a useful alternative to the junior hack-saw.

Sooner or later, hack-saw blades will need to be replaced. New blades have a roughness to them when the finger and thumb are run along the sides. Old blades lose that roughness and cut less effectively. To remove a blade from a junior hack-saw, compress the frame to release the blade lugs from the slots in the ends of the frame. With the frame compressed, fit the lugs of a new blade into the slots, ensuring that the blade's teeth point away from the handle. In knife-handle hack-saws, blades are removed by slackening the nut on the side of the frame. Again, the blade's teeth should point away from the handle.

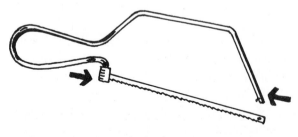

Figure 4.8   Removing a blade from a hack-saw.

Other saws

There are many other kinds of saw available. The teacher might find some of these useful for preparing materials to a suitable size and shape. For example, the handsaw is useful for cutting thick wood and boards to a usable size; the tenon-saw, having a metal stiffener along the back of the blade, can make neat, deep cuts. The technique used for cutting with a hack-saw applies to these saws too.

Sanding sticks, files and rasps

Sanding sticks, as their name suggests, are lengths of wood which have been dipped in adhesive and then in sand and left to harden. They are available in a range of cross-sections and are used like files. Their lives tend to be short, but they can be renewed fairly readily.

Rasps are coarse files used to shape wood. They remove material more quickly than abrasive papers and vary in size and shape, like the sanding stick. Perforated rasps have an action similar to a plane; when they are pushed forward, material is removed and curls through the holes on the upper surface.

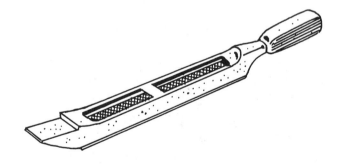

Figure 4.9   Perforated rasp.

Files are not as coarse as rasps and are used to shape and smooth metals. Like rasps, they come in a variety of sizes and shapes and are often available without handles. Handles may be obtained separately and the tangs of the file tapped into them. This needs to be done carefully as file metal is hard and brittle.

The vice

While the main purpose of a vice is to hold materials firmly, its use in connection with shaping metals, for example aluminium, should be mentioned here. When thin pieces of metal need to be bent into the required shape, they can be placed firmly in the vice along the bend line and hammered over to the required angle.

The hand drill

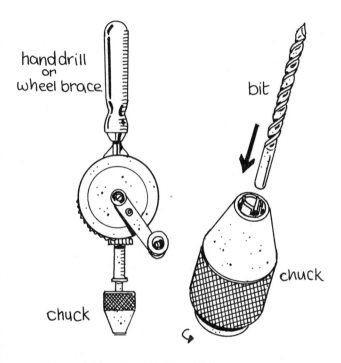

Figure 4.10   Hand drill and bit.

The hand drill or wheel brace is most often used for making holes for axles or screws. The part that actually makes the hole is called the *drill bit*. The part of the drill which holds the drill bit is the *chuck*. Turning the chuck anticlockwise by hand while the rest of the drill is held stationary retracts and opens a set of jaws in the chuck. The drill bit is placed in these jaws and the chuck turned clockwise to extend and close the jaws on to the bit. This must be done firmly or the bit will not turn in the wood when the drill handle is rotated. With the material held firmly, preferably by a clamp or a vice, the hole may now be drilled by gently pressing down with one hand on the main handle while turning the

crank clockwise with the other. A thick piece of scrap wood placed underneath the material is a wise precaution if table surfaces are not to be damaged. When children have difficulty in drilling in the right place, it helps to make a small dent at that point with a nail (or a punch, if one is available). Having drilled the hole, the natural inclination is to put the handle in reverse and attempt to unwind the drill bit from the material. However, this often results in releasing the bit, leaving it embedded in the hole. It is better to keep turning the drill in the same direction while pulling it out of the hole.

Selecting the correct drill bit to make a hole for an axle may present problems. One way to solve this is to try the axle in the drill storage holes and select the bit which is one size larger than the exact fit. If the axle is to go through card or thin plastic, it is more appropriate to use a hole punch or leather punch.

Beginners may find a drill stand, to which some makes of hand drill can be clipped, a useful aid. This takes the weight of the drill and holds it vertical while the child turns the crank. A piece of scrap wood should be placed under the material to reduce the risk of drilling into the base of the stand. If drills and a stand are being bought, check that at least one of your drills will fit the stand.

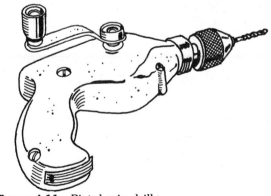

Figure 4.11   Pistol-grip drill.

Hand drills may be rather awkward tools for children and some might prefer those with a pistol-grip. An added advantage is that the cogs and gears are covered.

While many tools can be used with equal facility by right- and left-handed people, the hand drill can be an exception.

The gimlet

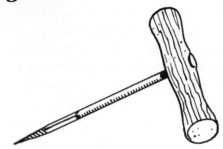

Figure 4.12 Gimlet.

The bradawl and gimlet are simple tools for making holes in wood to take screws and are used rather like an old-fashioned corkscrew. They may need more effort than the hand drill and since they make a hole of only one size, are more limited.

Joining

The way materials are joined depends on the materials being used and on whether the joint is intended to be permanent or temporary.

Adhesives

Adhesives can be used to provide a permanent or semi-permanent joint, provided the surfaces to be stuck together have large enough areas and are dry and free from dirt, dust, oil and grease. An adhesive commonly used in schools to join wood, paper, fabrics and a few plastics is the white, liquid adhesive, polyvinylacetate (PVA). Hot adhesive, dispensed by an electrically-heated glue gun, is also available in many schools. It may be used for the speedy joining of a wide range of materials, but it does melt some common plastics. With hot adhesive there is also the risk of scalds and local authority regulations should be checked regarding their policy towards the use of it. Even when regulations permit its use, the teacher needs to consider the capabilities of the child and ensure that there is adequate supervision. There is also a 'cool melt' version available and this might be a better alternative. It can be used on a wide range

of materials and is unlikely to melt plastics. Trigger glue guns are usually more expensive than thumb-operated guns but are easier to use. Of course, adhesives which contain dangerous solvents should be avoided.

When the contact area available for joining two materials is small, a joint stuck with adhesive will tend to be weak. It can be greatly strengthened by sticking another strip over the joint, reinforcing it with card or using wooden blocks.

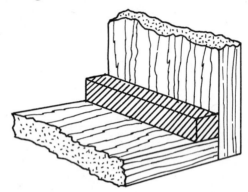

Figure 4.13 Reinforcing a joint.

Nails

Joining with nails is another way of making a permanent joint in suitable materials. Round, wire nails are useful for general joining tasks, except near the ends of pieces of wood where they may make it split. Oval nails reduce the likelihood of splitting, but are more likely to bend when hammered clumsily. If a nail must be inserted near the end of a piece of wood then a hole should be drilled first or the nail point blunted with a hammer. To increase the strength of a nailed joint, nails are often driven in at an angle so that it is more difficult to pull the pieces of wood apart.

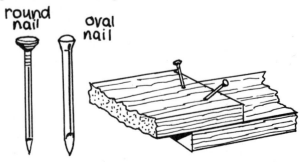

Figure 4.14 Round and oval nails and dovetail nailing for strength.

Hammers vary in size so it is possible to choose one which is not too heavy for children to use. When a hammer is too heavy, children tend to hold it near its head, something they may also do through ignorance. It is more efficient to hold the hammer at the end of the handle. This practice is also safer since it keeps the fingers of the hand holding the hammer well away from the nail. If the eye is kept on the nail rather than the hammer, the frequency of miss-hits is reduced.

Hammers also vary in function, although most can be used to drive a nail into wood. Hammers should never have loose heads; these can be tightened but it is important to use only the correct wedges.

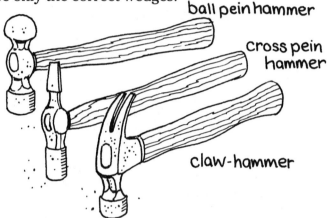

Figure 4.15 Some types of hammer.

Nuts and bolts

Nuts and bolts provide a means of joining materials which may need to be dismantled at some stage; in other words, they form a strong but temporary joint. Holes need to be drilled to take the bolt.

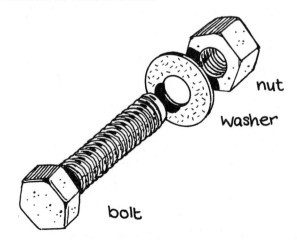

Figure 4.16 Bolt, nut and washer.

Screws

Screws also provide a way of making a strong, temporary joint. They are available in brass, aluminium and steel, the heads of the latter being harder and less likely to chew in inexpert hands. The slot in the head of a screw may be a straight cut across the head or in the shape of a cross. Screwdrivers are less likely to slip from the cross than from the straight slot. However, each kind needs its own, correctly fitting screwdriver. Screwdrivers need to be checked for signs of wear and damage. Worn or damaged ones should not be used.

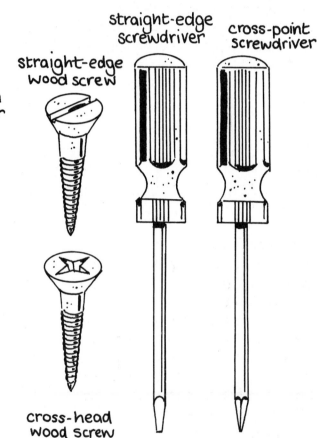

Figure 4.17 Screws and their screwdrivers.

Rivets

Rivets are mainly of use in permanently joining thin pieces of metal or hard plastics. Aluminium rivets are soft and easily peined over by a hammer, but the pop riveter takes even this small effort out of the task. Holes are first drilled in the materials, just big enough to take a rivet. A rivet is inserted in the riveter, pressed through the holes, then the handles are squeezed firmly. The pressure on the handle is released, the riveter pushed forwards again, and the process repeated, snapping the 'mandril' and leaving the rivet in place.

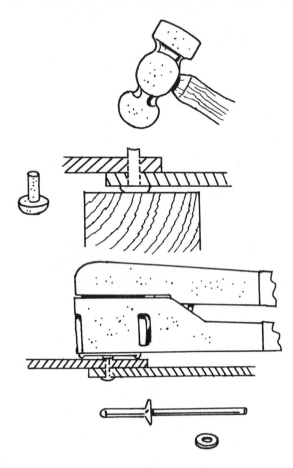

Figure 4.18 Two ways of riveting: using a soft aluminium rivet and pop riveting.

Miscellaneous ways of joining materials

There are many ways of joining materials which are specific to the particular material being used. For example, fabrics may be sewn permanently together, or joined temporarily with buttons or a zip.

Finishing

The operations described in the previous section may leave the surface of the artefact in an undesirable state. Perhaps it looks unattractive or risks damage from rust or rain. In short, it needs *finishing*. The first task, and sometimes the only one needed, is to clean the surfaces.

Abrasive papers

Abrasive papers are used to smooth edges, round corners, clean surfaces, and otherwise fine tune the components of an artefact. If the amount to be removed is small then sandpaper, a coarse, yellow abrasive, is suitable for wood and some plastics. Glass-paper, a fine, pale yellow abrasive, is less harsh and is used to produce a smooth finish. It is useful to have pieces of sandpaper and glass-paper fixed to blocks of wood with drawing-pins. They may be used as hand-held rubbing blocks or as fixed surfaces to rub materials on.

Emery is used to clean metal surfaces and is usually in the form of a stiff cloth with the abrasive on one side.

Where the amount of material to be removed is beyond the capabilities of abrasive papers then a file or rasp should be used instead.

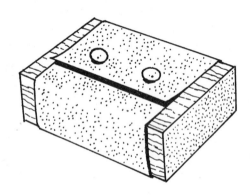

Figure 4.19 Sanding block.

Surface treatments

Water-based paints are adequate for most finishing tasks, but where artefacts are for outdoor use, their surfaces may need to be sealed to make them waterproof. One way to do this is to paint them with a primer and then give them a coat of a household, oil-based paint, but remember that this is not so readily cleaned from brushes, children and clothes.

PVA can be painted on to an object and allowed to dry to produce a transparent, protective coat. Solid, household wax polish is an alternative treatment. Rubbed into the surface of wood and over nail and screw heads, it will keep the weather at bay for a while. Where wood must stand the weather for some time, as with a bird table, the teacher may need to apply a suitable commercial preservative.

One quick and effective treatment is to place the artefact on a sheet of newspaper and spray it with a can of quick-drying paint. This should be done by the teacher, in a well-ventilated room and in accordance with the instructions on the can.

The tool kit

As has been described in Chapter Two, some good technology can be taught using the simplest of tools and materials, even when only using scissors, card and paper fasteners. However, children do need to experience working with other materials and these may require other tools to work them.

A short list of useful tools is provided below. It pays to buy good quality tools but bright and shiny is not always an indication of quality. Cheap screwdrivers, for instance, might look attractive in their bright chrome coating, but guard against those that are soft and lose their sharp edges the first time they are used.

Check tools regularly to make sure they are safe to use. Keep moving parts lightly oiled and occasionally wipe bare steel with an oily rag to prevent rusting. Good tools, well maintained, can last indefinitely.

Very useful tools
- Abrasive papers
- Bench hook
- Card snips
- File
- G-clamp
- Hammer
- Hand drill and drill bits
- Hole punch
- Junior hack-saw
- Pliers
- Rasp
- Safety rule
- Scissors
- Screwdriver (straight edge)
- Screwdriver (star point)

Useful tools
- Drill stand
- Glue gun
- Handsaw
- Pincers
- Tenon-saw
- Vice

Safety

Accidents have many causes, for example, lack of knowledge, lack of expertise, carelessness, bad habits, inappropriate clothing and inadequate protection, and inappropriate behaviour. They can occur in any kind of activity.

Planning for safety in technology means identifying the dangers and ensuring that the size of the risk is very small. Specific aspects to consider are:
- the place where the activity will take place – is it safe for the participants and onlookers?
- the equipment – are tools and materials kept secure when not in use? Is access limited to those intended for the children's use? Are the tools stored safely and maintained in a safe condition?
- ways of working – are children taught to use tools safely and to adopt safe practices?
- first aid – is there a simple kit readily available?
- safety rules – are these established and enforced?

Safety is not just something for children; teachers should set an example of good practice – accidents do not happen only to children. The Boy Scout and Girl Guide motto, 'Be prepared', is sound advice.

Chapter five

Planning, organising and managing technology education

Technology is well suited to the aims of primary education. First, the children are expected to do technology, that is, they are active participants in the process, the stages of which are as important as the end product. Second, through technology they gain first-hand experiences of skills and the applications of knowledge and understanding. Third, technology can cross traditional subject boundaries and integrate experiences, calling upon a wide range of skills, knowledge and understanding. Finally, technology can encourage the child to be a competent, independent person, taking increasing responsibility for his or her own learning.

There are many opportunities for technology in the primary classroom. The teacher's task is to help the children to recognise and use these opportunities, and hence to achieve the attainment targets of the National Curriculum. Such opportunities arise in:
• cross-curricular themes or topic work;
• familiar stories and rhymes;
• creative and imaginative play;
• meeting needs and solving problems which occur spontaneously in the classroom, school or neighbourhood.

What is important is that, 'Successful attitudes and practice are seldom the result of chance. They arise from schools' considering what they are trying to achieve, and carrying out a strategy for achieving it' (The Design Council, 1987).

The Department of Education and Science publication *Science 5–16: a statement of policy* (1985) identified ten principles which should be borne in mind when planning experiences for children in science. These principles can equally well be applied to technology education (or indeed, any area of the curriculum) as a starting point for planning. The ten principles are:
• breadth;
• balance;
• relevance;
• differentiation;
• equal opportunities;
• continuity;
• progression;
• links across the curriculum;
• teaching methods and approaches;
• assessment.

Interpreting these principles from the viewpoint of technology education, gives us ten criteria to be considered when planning technological experiences for children.

Breadth

All pupils should be introduced to a range of technological skills and processes, both in design and technology and in information technology. They should also learn about the technological applications of scientific knowledge and understanding, historical and cultural developments in technology and the social consequences of these developments.

Balance

All pupils should be able to continue their study of design and technology and information technology throughout their school lives. Technology education programmes should be designed to achieve a balance between the two components and offer a breadth of experience within each.

Relevance

Technology education should draw extensively on the everyday experiences of pupils, providing opportunities in relevant contexts to identify needs and solve problems. It should be aimed at preparing pupils as effectively as possible for life in an increasingly technological society.

As with many areas of experience in schools, the relevance of the task or activity is seldom made explicit. The children learn how to do things without appreciating why they are doing them.

Differentiation

The intellectual and practical demands made by technology education should be suited to the abilities of the pupils allowing the highest possible standards to be maintained for the most able pupils while catering fully for pupils unable to reach those standards. At the same time, it should provide the essential experience of a broad and balanced programme for all pupils.

Teachers catering for the individual differences of children are likely to make increasing use of open-ended activities, an approach especially suited to technology as an activity. In some ways planning for differentiation in technological activities can be relatively straightforward. The children may notice a need for a doorstop or for some way of storing wet paintings until they are dry. The teacher then turns these real problems over to the children themselves to solve. Each child will interpret the task and respond accordingly, working at his or her own level of skill and understanding. If some 30 children worked on a problem independently there could, feasibly, be 30 different solutions to that problem. The nature of technology as a process enables tasks to be interpreted differently by individuals. However, such tasks must be planned with progression in mind, as described in Chapters Eight, Nine and Eleven.

Another thing to think about when planning for differentiation is how tasks, problems or challenges are presented to the children. Some general rules when planning technology might include:

• plan structured tasks which are challenging yet achievable;

• introduce new tasks and activities to the whole class beforehand;

• keep oral and written instructions or directions simple, so aiding independence;

• present instructions to non-readers using pictures or tape recorded directions;

• communicate written tasks (for example, worksheets or cards) in an attractive and appealing way, using short sentences, simple vocabulary and pictures beside key words;

• ensure that all pupils are familiar with the vocabulary (use personal wordlists, dictionaries, labelled diagrams or other suitable forms of support);

• allow mixed ability groups so that more able children can help their classmates;

• if possible, allow multi-age grouping, so that older children can tutor younger ones (cross-age or peer tutoring);

• use other adults, school auxiliaries or parents whenever possible, either to work with other groups or to work with children involved in a technology task;

• have expectations appropriate to individual pupils and recognise all pupils' successes.

One system which lends itself well to planning for differentiation is the *learning centre* or *workstation*. The main purpose of a workstation is to provide opportunities for enrichment of a topic or theme. It enables a child to work independently or with a friend and explore experiences, ideas of interest or new challenges. Workstations have an added advantage in that they also allow teachers to control access to resources. (Workstations are described more fully at the end of the chapter on page 74).

Equal opportunities

Technology education should give genuinely equal opportunities to both girls and boys and ensure that both find tasks relevant and interesting.

The popular view that home economics is for girls and wood and metal work are for boys is anachronistic. Technology is a new subject which aims to offer *all* pupils an equal experience of inventing things and opportunities to solve material problems. Initially, boys and girls might not work well together on technological tasks and so friendship groups or single-sex groups might be allowed. Later, mixed pairs can be introduced to encourage co-operation.

Cultural diversity is another aspect of providing equal opportunities in technology. The contributions of different cultures can also enhance the learning experiences of all children. Opportunities to use experiences from other cultures should not be restricted to classrooms where there are children from those cultures. Aspects of food technology, environmental planning and fabric design can all benefit by considering the beliefs, practices and aesthetics of other cultures.

Continuity

Children transfer from first to middle school or from primary to secondary school and, if what has been achieved is not to be wasted, links are needed between the schools. The organisation of primary schools is very varied. Even those schools which profess to have similar philosophies and aims are often very different in practice. Some aspects of organisation are not within the control of the school, for example, local education authority policies on primary education and in-service training support for staff. Often there are internal factors, such as resource allocation and allocation of responsibilities which influence philosophy. These have implications for curricular organisation and so it is essential that curriculum continuity is considered when planning programmes of work and deciding how progress will be monitored and recorded. Most infant, junior and secondary schools (or first, middle and high schools) have structures in place intended to aid transition from one phase of education to the next. These are often concerned with reducing to a minimum the emotional disruption that such transitions can cause children. A five to sixteen National Curriculum makes it essential that curriculum disruption does not occur. Some strategies which can be used include:

• Visits by the older pupils in the infant, first or primary school to that in the next phase. They could be engaged in a technological activity while at the same time becoming familiar with the new environment.

• Visits by pupils from the junior, middle or secondary school to work alongside younger pupils, in a peer-tutoring capacity. This may work well in technological activities.

• Technology fairs involving all the schools in an area, with common problems to solve and challenges to meet.

• Joint staff meetings to share ideas and consider issues such as planning, record keeping and assessment.

Progression

Programmes of work in technology should be designed to give progressively greater capability in both design and technology and information technology. The complex issue of progression in technology is explored in depth in Chapter Eight.

Links across the curriculum

Almost any area of the curriculum, or of a child's life, can provide situations and contexts for technological activity. Technology, therefore, may enhance integration of the curriculum – something of great value since it reduces the tendency of children to compartmentalise their experiences according to subject labels. The knowledge and understanding used in design and technology is drawn from a wide range of experience and, of course, the programmes of study of the National Curriculum subjects. Similarly, information technology is a tool which may be used in

almost any area of the curriculum. Many of the dimensions, themes and skills identified in the document *The Whole Curriculum* (NCC 'Curriculum Guidance 3', 1990) are fundamental to technology. For example, in the definition of enterprise, as outlined within the theme 'Economic and Industrial Understanding', are many of the competencies associated with team work and co-operation which are developed in technology. The skill areas of problem solving and communication can also be developed in technology. By its nature, technology is catholic in its taste and recognises few boundaries.

Teaching methods and approaches

Technology is a practical activity and should be taught, at all stages, in ways which emphasise this fact.

The teacher's role

As a general rule, children are more motivated when given a choice in what they do and a variety in ways of learning. They also learn well from first-hand experience and through interaction with others. What is the teacher's role in this?

Ultimately the teacher should aim for children to be able to identify needs and opportunities in technology for themselves and carry out technology procedures of their own design to achieve solutions. The teacher's role will alter as these competencies develop.

Leader
As leader the teacher should facilitate free talk in which he or she guides the children's progress, perhaps providing a design and technology brief or instructions, or by leading a planning session.

Questioner
The teacher should use key questions to focus attention on important aspects of the activity and direct observations and ideas towards possible ways forward.

Assessor

As assessor the teacher appraises ideas, suggests designs or solutions and, through questions and discussion, leads the children to explain and justify what they are doing.

Challenger

As challenger the teacher asks open-ended questions or challenges the children to do something, perhaps focusing on particular processes, strategies, materials or applications of knowledge, gradually widening the experience.

Observer

As observer the teacher should stand back and observe as children generate their own problems, ideas, solutions and tasks.

Approaches

When planning for any area of the primary curriculum, two main approaches are possible. One is to develop a subject-based or core curriculum, in which areas of the curriculum are taught very much as separate subjects. There are some advantages to using this approach. First, it is possible to plan a programme for technology which ensures a progression in skills, knowledge and understanding, developed through a continuous programme of experience from reception to top junior classes. Second, it is possible to focus upon particular aspects of technology within this programme, for example to teach a particular skill, to use particular materials or to develop particular artefacts, systems or environments with specific age ranges. Third, it is possible to plan and manage the necessary materials and resources fairly readily throughout the school. However, there are also several disadvantages. The curriculum can lack flexibility and spontaneity and children have little choice in what they do and when they do it. Since the whole class might do technology together, there is a heavy demand on resources. Such a curriculum tends to be divided into slots whereby the children are unable to spend longer than planned on tasks, and opportunities to link experiences are often missed. Tasks risk

being seen as irrelevant exercises with little long-term value.

The second approach is to plan through topics, themes or projects. As mentioned earlier, technology can arise naturally in most areas of the curriculum so this approach is not inimical to it. The topic, theme or project is usually one chosen by the teacher, who then uses his or her knowledge of the children and the topic concerned to identify specific technological activities. For example, a topic on transport might involve the children in using spreadsheets and collecting information about traffic going past the school, for storage and retrieval using a computer data-handling package. They might then be asked to design and make wheeled vehicles which will travel across the hall under their own power. Alternatively, the teacher could outline a topic and, through discussion with the children, identify a number of possible tasks to carry out, problems to solve or needs which must be satisfied. The children then select the task or problem which most interests them, perhaps modifying it to suit themselves. For example, in a project on 'shopping', and following a visit to the local supermarket, the children might identify problems to do with advertising and the movement of goods or design a survey to determine who buys different products. The teacher may have identified a packaging problem or initiated a survey to find where the children's family do their weekly shopping. All these ideas can go into the pot for the children to consider and choose from.

As with the core approach, there are both advantages and disadvantages to this method. On the one hand, it can promote realistic, integrated learning experiences, drawn from many areas of the curriculum. It can help make explicit the relevance of various experiences by linking them to the immediate environment of the child. It allows for freedom and flexibility, providing opportunities for the children to contribute personal interests and ideas. It facilitates small group and individual work, thus reducing demands on limited resources. It

also allows individuals to work at their own pace and at their own level, thus facilitating a differentiated programme. On the other hand, not every topic judged appropriate for the primary classroom will contain opportunities for technology and so it is difficult to ensure that breadth, balance, progression and continuity are maintained throughout the primary years. Unless the programme for the whole school is planned co-operatively there might well be unnecessary duplication or omission of experiences. It is necessary to analyse experiences carefully and keep detailed records of topics, to ensure all the appropriate elements of the programmes of study for *Technology in the National Curriculum* are covered.

As is usually the case, the solution would seem to be a balance between the two approaches, which builds upon the advantages of both. Short-term, timetabled activities could be used to develop specific skills and competencies, while longer-term projects could give the children more freedom to explore ideas and opportunities. Thus time could be used flexibly, from half-a-day per week of technology at some times of the year through to half-termly projects or even one or two day concentrated technology-challenge events at the end of the school year.

Classroom organisation

There is a wide range of ways to organise the class for technology. Some teachers will prefer to have the *whole class* doing technology at the same time. At times, this is the more difficult way, since it makes great demands on resources. There may be only one computer, materials for control technology may be limited (see Chapter Thirteen), and for design and technology there may be few tool kits. However, it is possible on occasions to have the whole class involved, for example, in doing paper technology or when a teacher wants to demonstrate how to do something (use a particular tool perhaps or to demonstrate a particular skill). Reporting back and explaining work in progress or demonstrating end-products can also be done as a whole class. If this way is used, it is recommended that furniture be moved so that children can gather around the demonstrator. This has an added advantage with younger children, who need to be close and feel involved otherwise they may lose interest.

Often children will work on technology in *small groups* of perhaps four or five pupils. This is particularly appropriate when a range of resources are available. The teacher can organise the class into workgroups, which can be selected in various ways. Friendship groups are a good starting point for technology, as task sharing and co-operation can be more smoothly facilitated. However, such groups will often be single-sex and there are occasions when co-operation between the sexes is to be encouraged. Mixed ability

groups can also be used to encourage peer tutoring. In some schools, peer tutoring is taken further by having older pupils work with younger children in a co-operative way. An extra adult (auxiliary or parent) is also useful when working in this way. With this method of organisation the teacher still has the option of having the whole class do technology at the same time, on the same or on a variety of different activities.

When children are working *as* a group (as opposed to *in* a group), they sometimes work better if they are assigned roles or special jobs to do within their groups. These could be allocated by the teacher or appointed by the children themselves. For example, in a group of four children, one would be the chairperson, leading the group and reading task briefs. A second member of the group could act as recorder, noting ideas and information collected. The third member could have responsibility for collecting together and later returning the resources needed. The final member would be the spokesperson for the group, giving an oral report on their activities. All members of the group would carry out a specific part of the activity itself. If the groups were maintained, they could rotate their roles. Such a structure offers children real opportunities for co-operative decision making and appreciation of the importance of teamwork and feedback.

Some teachers might decide to have children working individually or in pairs. In an ideal world, every child in the class would be able to manipulate materials and equipment individually or with a partner whenever they wished. Primary classrooms are seldom ideal. However, this can be helped by establishing technology areas in the classroom, which would include:

- a relatively dust-free area for information technology;
- a display area which can be changed regularly and provide stimulus;
- a clean technology area for food and fabric technology;
- a technology area for working with water, paints, clay, wood and so on;

• a storage area for the equipment needed for technology.

Obviously such areas may be dual purpose, used for other activities as well as for technological ones. The idea of technology areas is developed further in the section on technology workstations (see page 74).

Managing children

As with any experience we offer children, it is important that they know what is expected of them. It is also important that the teacher's attitude towards technology in the classroom is such that it is perceived as an important and valuable experience. It should never be seen as merely a pastime or something which can be interrupted for 'more important' tasks. Once engaged in a technological activity, the child should be allowed to complete the task. In planning technological activities a teacher should have some idea of roughly how long it will take, but be sufficiently flexible to allow slower children extra time if they need it. Similarly, children who work faster might need some extension activities or purposeful alternatives, perhaps working in a different technology area or at the workstation. Teachers also need to give children time to learn and practice new skills and procedures if they are to be used with competency and efficiency.

The teacher will need to consider:
• *Safety* – tasks using tools or computer-controlled equipment will need to be carried out away from the main classroom traffic routes and uncluttered by personal belongings such as bags and clothing. Technology areas should be well-lit.
• *Furniture* – ordinary tables are likely to be in use and will need to be washable and covered to protect their surfaces. Again, they should be cleared of unnecessary materials for technology activities.
• *Resources* – these should be stored and organised in such a way that the children themselves can access and replenish them without it becoming yet another task for the teacher. There should be sufficient variety to allow children's ideas to be developed and the children should know what is available, where to find it and how to use it.

Assessment

Progress in technology should be assessed in ways which recognise the importance of the skills and processes of technology as well as the ability to draw upon and apply knowledge and understanding from other areas of the curriculum.

Assessment is obviously an important aspect of teaching and learning which is discussed more fully in Chapter Six.

Planning technology tasks

In primary classrooms, programmes of work are seldom spontaneous. Primary teachers usually make some sort of plan or topic web for a new block of work. Such a plan will also serve to identify opportunities for design and technology or information technology. A topic on 'transport', for example, could provide opportunities for designing and making self-propelled vehicles and the collection, storage and retrieval of data on traffic outside the school, using spreadsheets and a data-handling package. The next step is to translate the ideas and opportunities into design and technology or information technology tasks or activities. Technological activity planning sheets (see Figures 5.1 and 5.2) can be used for this purpose. Planning sheets help to identify the various attributes of design and technology and information technology to be offered to the children. They would normally be completed before the children attempt an activity. An example of a completed planning sheet for design and technology is given in Figure 5.1.

All possible objectives are unlikely to be achieved in any single task and so not all lines will be completed on any one planning sheet. Taken together and over a period of time, the planning sheets provide an overview of the progression and continuity the teacher is seeking. The planning sheet can also become the basis for assessing the children's achievements, as described in Chapter Six.

The technology workstation

Workstations are not a new idea. In the United States of America the use of workstations is common in many elementary schools. A workstation is a place where several children at a time can work independently, using instructions, activities and resources found at that place. They can be established for any area of the curriculum or for cross-curricular topic work, and are designed so that children can choose which tasks they wish to do and work at their own pace and in their own way. The time at the workstation can be directed by the teacher or chosen by the children, as can whether the child works alone, with a partner or with his or her group. An example of a technology workstation is given in Figure 5.3.

At the workstation the children will find not only the resources which might be needed but also an assortment of worksheets and cards. These would include:
• structured task sheets, suggesting things children might do in design and technology or information technology;
• planning sheets, to be completed by individuals or groups;
• plan-do-review sheets, for individuals to complete to identify their ideas and contributions to a task;
• challenge sheets, suggesting open-ended problems linked to the particular topic or theme under study.

There would also be a background display of storybooks, poems, posters and other artefacts and resource materials related to the topic or theme being studied and examples of the children's own work. This would serve to establish the topic or theme, focus attention and motivate the children. Children who are non-readers could listen to stories and poems using earphones and a tape recorder. Directions could be given in a similar way.

A record book could also be left at the workstation in which the children record when they use the workstation, which sheets or cards they completed and any other information related to their work.

Simple, overall instructions would tell the children how to use the workstation properly (the number of children using it at any one time, returning tools and resources to the station after use, topping up resources, and so on).

Design and technology activity planning sheet

Date: <u>Nov./Dec.</u>   Class: <u>Year 1</u>   Topic: <u>Shopping</u>

Activity: <u>Using limited materials, design and make a</u> carrier bag to carry three items from shop.

	Resources
Artefact/system/environment <u>Artefact</u> - paper carrier bag, with handle(s) to carry three items from shop corner.	Collection of items (eg tea bag box, plastic bottle and sweet bag).
Working with materials – Materials limited; introducing economic constraints; recognition that resources are not limitless. – Previous experience of: working with paper (strength of different types; folding; tubes; carrying loads); fixing with tape, clips, etc.	Scissors 2 paper clips 10 cm adhesive tape large (A1) sheet of news print.
Satisfying needs/addressing opportunities – Need introduced to class as teacher's problem- have carrier bag containing three objects on which handles have snapped. – Can they work in pairs; develop some ideas; select; design and make; evaluate. – Aesthetic- look at 'real' bags for ideas to decorate	Bag with objects -handle snapped. Collection of carrier bags.
Generating/developing/ communicating ideas – Talking to one another about the problem, after inital stimulus from teacher; describe to another pair what their ideas were and why they chose a particular one; use drawings to help.	Designing sheets.

Figure 5.1   Design area and technology activity planning sheet.

Information technology activity planning sheet

Date: _____ Class: _____ Topic: _____ Activity: _____	**Resources**
Developing ideas and communicating information	
Handling information	
Modelling	
Measurement and control	
Applications and effects	

Figure 5.2 Information technology activity planning sheet.

When setting up a technology workstation, the teacher needs to think about the physical environment of the classroom. Is there enough space for several children to access the station at any one time? What will be the main traffic routes to and from the station? Can the computer be used where it is or will it have to be moved? Is there room for displaying stimulating materials, both on walls and other flat surfaces?

Providing, storing and restocking materials will also need to be considered. If the children are involved in open-ended activities, the teacher will not be sure how quickly different materials will be used. Much of what is needed can be brought in by the children themselves (for example, tubes, boxes, fabric scraps and so on). How will these be stored so that they are easily accessible and logically sorted and labelled? Plastic trays or boxes from commercial suppliers are one solution. Plastic ice-cream cartons or plastic vegetable trays from the local supermarket are a cheap alternative. For small items plastic cutlery trays are also useful. If tools are stored in a crate or box, a contents list should be fixed to the side for the children to check after use. If tools are stored on a horizontal or vertical board, it is useful to have tool silhouettes to show which tool belongs where and provide an easy check for missing tools. Consumable items should be listed separately and kept in stock (for example, jelutong, adhesive sticks for glue guns, sticky tape). Once the station is up and running, the children themselves can take responsibility for maintaining it.

Figure 5.3 Technology workstation.

Chapter six

Monitoring progress: the assessment and recording of learning

Teachers are constantly making judgements about the work in their classrooms. These may be subjective impressions; an experienced teacher who knows the class well can often sense when things are going well or badly. But often, such judgements are based on more systematic methods of gathering information, that is, *assessment*. Information for assessment can be gathered by both teachers and pupils. In evaluating technology the teacher needs to examine three aspects:

• *planning* what and how technological experiences are being provided;

• *assessing* the pupils' all-round technological development through the planned experiences, which means knowing where they started and where they stopped;

• *recording* in some clear, concise and convenient form what has been planned, experienced and achieved.

Yet, 'Few primary schools have a consistent policy for assessing practical and activity-based learning, or keep records of pupils' achievements in activities related to design' (The Design Council, 1987).

Work should be evaluated and this evaluation should be an integral part of normal classroom life. 'Good activities are based on good observation and assessment which also provides evidence for records. The context of the task, the resources, the challenges provided, and the teacher's style in questioning and supporting the child, will all contribute to the quality of the opportunities for assessment' (ASE, 1990).

Assessment

Some teachers will teach technology as a part of a cross-curricular topic, such as transport. Others will prefer to develop technological capabilities through separate technology lessons. Whichever approach is used, the teacher will need to assess the learning of the children in order to 'ensure that individual pupils are working at the appropriate level for any given attainment target and programme of study . . . inform those with an interest . . . about individual pupil's progress . . . build up a bank of relevant information about a pupil's progress . . . on which to draw in the context of any discussions about the level that pupil is judged to have reached at the end of the key stage' (DES, 1990).

In this way assessment has three major aims:
• Assessment *evaluates* formatively and diagnostically. That is, it provides the teacher with information which:
  (a) is used to match experiences to pupils' needs, interests and abilities;
  (b) helps to determine what the next stage in the learning process will be;
  (c) aids the setting of goals;
  (d) gives feedback on performance.
• Assessment *informs*. It helps the teacher to:
  (a) talk to the children about their progress;

(b) advise the children's parents and other interested adults about progress; .
(c) provide information for the children's subsequent teachers.

• Assessment *summarises*. It provides an overall picture of achievement, of what individuals or groups know, understand and can do.

It is also important to remember that assessment produces information which is as much a reflection of teacher provision as of pupil performance. Any assessment of pupils must be matched by evaluation of the experiences offered to them and the teaching and learning strategies employed. This means looking at what has been planned and how the experiences were organised and managed.

As far as *Technology in the National Curriculum* is concerned, assessment is based upon the teacher's professional judgement about each pupil's level of attainment. There are several sources for guidance on National Curriculum assessment. The National Curriculum requirements, as outlined in the *DES Circular 3/90*, have already been mentioned. The full details of this are published by the School Examination and Assessment Council (SEAC). However, more general sources are available, for example SEAC's *Guide to Teacher Assessment* pack and the joint publication of the various associations for mathematics, English and science, *Teacher Assessment – making it work for the primary school* (Association for Science Education, 1990). These offer good advice on assessment, much that is sensible (and realistic in the light of current demands on primary teachers) and easily interpreted from the perspective of different areas of the curriculum.

What is to be assessed in design and technology?

It would be easy in design and technology to look only at the end-product; the artefact, system or environment.

Technology education however, is *process* oriented and a major focus for assessment will be on the processes, strategies and skills which the children will need to develop and use competently. These, however, cannot be developed and practised in a vacuum. They must be experienced in a context which requires the acquisition and application of appropriate knowledge and understanding. Finally, what a child is *able* to do is often different from what that child will *choose* to do. The former is determined partly by skills, knowledge and understanding while the latter is dependent upon personal qualities, such as interests. It is useful for the teacher to know what the children can understand and apply, what they can do and what they would prefer to do. In technology, processes, knowledge, understanding and personal qualities should become the focus of assessment.

Processes, strategies and skills

In design and technology pupils will be developing and using a wide range of processes, strategies and skills. Few of them will be unique to technology.

At the most basic level, *fine and gross motor skills* such as picking up and holding a pencil or nail, or cutting with scissors, hand-eye co-ordination, and general manual dexterity are developed through technology. *Mathematical skills* like estimating and measuring are needed. *Manipulative skills* are developed when handling a range of tools. These basic practical skills are practised when children develop their technological capabilities as identified in the programmes of study as the children design and make artefacts, systems and environments. They need to be used regularly to develop and maintain the level of capability required.

Because children often need to work co-operatively in technology, there is a need for discussion between themselves and with adults. This develops their *talking and listening skills*. *Reading and writing skills* are developed in seeking out information and resources, using games and simulations, word processing and writing about their experiences when tackling technological

problems. These provide opportunities for vocabulary development, as issues relating to designing and making are discussed. For example, 'As David and Steven tried to find a piece of wood to pull their car across the table, appropriate vocabulary developed: too big and too small were rapidly discarded in favour of heavier and lighter as the distinction between size and weight was clarified' (Williams and Jinks, 1985).

Through design and technology children are encouraged to develop their own *strategies* for meeting needs and solving problems. These include evaluating ideas and solutions and rethinking and reassessing the problem in the light of success or failure. By providing effective, ready links between areas of the primary curriculum children are encouraged to recognise how the different areas relate to one another. They draw upon the experiences in these different areas to recognise needs and solve design and technology problems. This requires them to observe accurately and to analyse situations. In their search for information they must value the information they collect, think logically and put ideas into

sequence. The capacity to imagine artefacts, systems and environments and to use signs and symbols to represent these images may also be developed.

Knowledge and understanding

'Pupils should be taught to draw on their knowledge and skills in other subjects, particularly the foundation subjects of science, mathematics and art, to support their designing and making activities. These activities should also reflect their growing understanding of the needs and beliefs of other people and cultures, now and in the past' (*Technology in the National Curriculum,* page 19).

The teacher will need to know what specific *facts, ideas, concepts, laws, principles* and *terminology* each child has acquired. Recall of such knowledge is readily checked through oral questions or written tests. However, the mere acquisition of knowledge is not sufficient in itself. The aim is for understanding and application, especially where that application is in a new context. For example, when making a model of a house from large cardboard boxes the child might wish to put a light inside one of the rooms. From science the child might know that a complete circuit is needed for a current to flow. That is, the child can state the rule. But if the child does not understand it sufficiently well to set up the circuit and make the bulb light, then he or she cannot apply the knowledge. It is this last step which is crucial for design and technology – the application of knowledge and understanding from other areas of the curriculum. It is, of course, this capability which makes much of our education worthwhile. In practice, children will often work in groups and this can obscure the actual knowledge, understanding and application of individuals. It can be difficult to identify clearly each child's contribution.

Since much of the knowledge and understanding comes from science, it is often difficult to separate science and technology in the primary classroom. Some aspects of science and technology are described in Section Three. Knowledge and understanding will also be drawn from other sources, such as business and economic influences, health and safety education, the creative and expressive arts, and social and environmental education.

Personal qualities and attitudes

The role of technology education in fostering and developing *personal qualities* and *attitudes* is also important. Technology can bring a range of personal, social and cultural dimensions to learning.

Children can be observed as they work to see what attitudes and personal qualities are shown in their behaviour. This observation is, of necessity, informal but it helps to have a check-list against which to note development. The list would include:
• aesthetic appreciation;
• co-operation;
• creativity;
• enterprise;
• imagination;
• independence;
• ingenuity;
• initiative;
• leadership;
• organisation;
• perseverance;
• persistence;
• reliability;
• responding to the ideas of others;
• responsibility to self and others;
• valuing the views of others.

The development of positive attitudes and qualities is reflected in academic performance, in the non-academic aspects of school life and in out-of-school activities.

In order to monitor processes, knowledge and understanding, and personal qualities simple check-lists can be used. Examples of such check-lists are shown in Figures 6.1 and 6.2. When assessing progress, it is advisable to limit the number of criteria to about five or six at the most. With a group of five older children, five criteria are manageable. With very young children, this may well be limited to only two or three criteria.

For example, in a topic on 'shopping', a class of six-year-olds could be asked to design and make a paper carrier bag to carry 1kg of potatoes, using limited materials. The teacher might look for the following five things:
• Does the child put forward an idea to test?
• Can the child describe how he or she is working?

Design and technology: criteria check-list

Date: _____ Class: _____

Topic: _____

	Activity				
	1	2	3	4	5

A. Processes, strategies, skills:
- Fine and gross motor skills;
- manipulative skills;
- mathematical skills;
- communication skills;
- thinking skills;
- problem solving strategies;
- process: generating ideas;
  - planning;
  - designing;
  - making;
  - evaluating.

B. Knowledge and understanding
- Mathematical;
- scientific: forces;
  - energy;
  - materials;
  - hydraulics;
  - pneumatics;
- technological: control;
  - structures;
  - systems.
- historical;
- social/cultural.

C. Personal qualities and attitudes
- Aesthetic appreciation;
- co-operation;
- creativity/imagination;
- independence/initiative;
- perserverence/persistance;
- responding to ideas of others;
- responsibility.

Figure 6.1

Information technology: criteria check-list

Date: _____ Class: _____ Topic: _____

	Activity			
1	2	3	4	5

A. Processes, strategies, skills:
• Fine and gross motor skills;
• communication skills;
• thinking skills;
• problem solving skills;
• developing ideas;
• handling information;
• modelling/simulating;
• measurement/control.

B. Knowledge and understanding:
• Curricular links:　mathematics;
　　　　　　　　　English;
　　　　　　　　　science;
　　　　　　　　　art;
　　　　　　　　　geography;
　　　　　　　　　history;
　　　　　　　　　religious education;
　　　　　　　　　music;
　　　　　　　　　other areas.
• Contexts/applications.

C. Personal qualities and attitudes:
• Aesthetics;
• co-operation;
• creativity/imagination;
• independence;
• initiative;
• persistence;
• responsibility;
• valuing views of others.

Figure 6.2

• Does the child draw upon his or her knowledge of the properties of paper?
• Will the child co-operate with a partner?
• Can the child evaluate the outcome?

Ten-year-olds, working on the same topic, might decide to set up a shop corner for the reception classroom, for which they have to design and make the various structures and artefacts. This time the criteria might be:
• Does the child select from a range of their ideas according to available materials and resources?
• Does the child contribute to the designing of the shop?
• Does the child take responsibility for making a particular part of the shop?
• Does the child use a range of tools safely and responsibly?
• Can the child evaluate his or her contribution to the whole?

In assessing for the National Curriculum, these criteria, like those listed earlier, should relate closely to the statements of attainment. A *technology task assessment grid* (see Figure 6.3) is useful for this. Criteria selected from the above check-lists or alternatives to meet specific needs are listed down the side of the chart and the children involved in the activity are listed along the top. Brief comments are written in the boxes on the grid. Such an assessment grid can be used throughout a project, whether it lasts for one lesson or a whole term. Alternatively, the sheet could be used for just one child, with stages in the project listed along the top rather than other children's names. This information can later be transferred to a summary record sheet, as a recording wheel (see Figure 6.10). Comments accumulate and reflect on the child's performance over time.

What is to be assessed in information technology?

Much of what has been said about design and technology applies equally to information technology. However, there is not always concrete evidence of information technology activity which can be put into a child's portfolio for future reference. What is common to both is the process-based approach. Through information technology children will be developing skills, drawing upon knowledge and understanding acquired through other areas of experience and developing desirable attitudes.

Processes, strategies and skills

Information technology aids the development of fine and gross motor skills and hand-eye co-ordination. Using keyboards, whether overlay or QWERTY, obviously requires accuracy and precision. Communication skills are enhanced as the children use information technology. When using word processing they will be developing reading and writing skills. Through cross-curricular games, modelling or simulations and when planning

Task assessment grid

Date: <u>Nov. 26th</u>   Activity: Designing and making carrier bag

	Kellie	Sam	Rajeev	Amy	
Suggests what might be done. AT (1b)	Saw problem of carrying things; commented on need for a bag. ✓	— ✗	Picked up Kellie's point – suggested asking Mrs H. ✓	— ✗	
Develops design proposal as picture. AT2 (2a)	Produced three possibilities. ✓	Contributed idea to ⬦ of chip bag. ?	Drew carefully; drawing of tyre. ✓	No contribution ✗	
Uses knowledge of materials (paper). AT3 (2a)	Reference to paper folding work – folded handle.	Said paper would not be strong enough – would tear.	—	—	
Describes what has been done. AT4 (1a)	Good – sequenced task; explained reason for folding handle.	— ✗	Quiet let Amy talk. ✗	Quite good description of what Rajeev did. ?	
Discusses how satisfactory results are. AT4 (2a)	—	—	—	—	
Works co-operatively with partner.	Dominated task – very much in control.	—	—	Let Rajeev do the making.	

Figure 6.3

strategies for action, the children will be talking and listening to one another, sharing ideas and using problem solving skills. Simulations and computer modelling help to develop thinking skills further. Using spreadsheets and handling data encourages logical and analytical thinking and pattern recognition.

Knowledge and understanding
Using a software package, such as *Golden Eagle* (Cambridge University Press), the pupils are asked to draw upon their knowledge and understanding of living things and food chains. They use this knowledge and understanding to predict patterns and put forward simple, testable hypotheses suggesting why populations are changing and how to alter events. The control of Big Trak or a Roamer requires that the children draw upon and develop a range of mathematical knowledge and understanding in connection with number, direction, angles, estimation and measurement.

Attitudes
Some desirable attitudes develop through shared tasks and co-operative behaviour. These are as for design and technology, but would obviously need to be recorded in a different way. A suggestion for a simple check-list to use when observing children is given in Figure 6.2.

What strategies can be used to assess technological capabilities?
'The assessment process itself should not determine what is to be taught and learned. It should be the servant, not the master, of the curriculum . . . It therefore needs to be incorporated systematically into teaching strategies and practices at all levels' (DES, 1988).

The judgements made about children's progress in any area of the curriculum are made by collecting evidence in a variety of ways. These might include:
- observing the children at work;
- discussing their activities with them;
- examining the products of their work;
- setting specific tasks (practical or written);
- involving children in their own assessment.

Observing children at work
Teachers constantly observe children as they work. This observation is usually discreet, even clandestine, but is also purposeful. Is Jane using her ruler correctly? Can Matthew punctuate his writing with speech marks? Will James let his partner have a turn using the computer? Is Susan choosing the materials sensibly for her model? Is Terry's work better than last time?

Questions like these are at the heart of assessment. Objectives are usually stated during planning. These objectives identify what children are expected to achieve in terms of:
- what they will know or understand;
- what they will be able to do;
- how they will behave and interact.

For example, the task objectives might be that by the end of the activity, the pupils will have:
- learned that the . . .;
- understood how to . . .;
- described what happened when . . .;
- planned how to . . .;
- measured the materials for . . .;
- acted responsibly with tools when . . .;

• evaluated the . . .;
• applied knowledge of . . .;
• worked co-operatively with . . . .

The verbs used can become the criteria for assessing the children's success or otherwise as they work. Thus, with the objectives listed above, the assessment criteria become:
• Has he or she learned that the . . .?
• Does he or she understand how to . . .?
• Can he or she describe what he or she did when . . .?
• Did he or she plan how to . . .?
• Could he or she measure the materials for . . .?
• Did he or she act responsibly with tools when . . .?
• Did he or she evaluate the . . .?
• Was he or she able to apply knowledge of . . .?
• Did he or she work co-operatively with . . .?

When observing children it is better to note only the big things and not the minutiae. This limits the number of criteria to five or six. Sometimes a task assessment grid might not be available. A notebook, with one page per child could be kept to hand, in which important occurrences, for instance, something the child says or does, could be noted. It is useful to date such notes. These become a diary-profile of each child, which could be supplemented with samples of children's work.

Often, it will not be possible to spend very much time sitting with a child or group. One possible strategy is to dip into their activity, perhaps spending five minutes with them at key times. This might be during the planning stage, while they are discussing their problem-solving strategies, as they enter their data into a computer spreadsheet or while they are evaluating outcomes. If a teacher wishes to monitor the whole of the activity then leaving a tape recorder running might help. Asking children to make comments on tape is also feasible. Print outs from the computer, such as data sheets, prose or other computer-generated products, will also help in the assessment.

Discussing activities with children

Talking with children as they work is useful. What the children say is as important as what they do. Teachers talk with them as they work, not only to determine progress, but also to give the children some feedback and positive reinforcement. This talk has two important forms: closed questions and open questions. Closed questions typically produce short answers focused on specific pieces of information. For example, Which tool did you use for cutting the plastic sheet? Why did you use that one? Who did you talk to in order to collect the information about the shops they used? Why did you choose them? What instructions did you need to make the turtle turn right? How would you make it return to the starting point?

A deeper insight into children's thinking and reasoning skills is gained by asking more open questions. For example, What could you have done if a hack-saw had not been available? How could you get your buggy to move like the turtle? or How do you think you could stop the foxes eating all the hares?

With infants, who have more limited recording skills, questioning is an important way of collecting evidence for assessment. Whatever the kind of question, it is important that children are given enough time to answer questions in their own way.

Another strategy is to listen to children talking. Pupil to pupil talk provides insights into thinking which might be missed when using preconceived questions.

Examining the products of their work

The range of products from technological activities can be large. For assessment purposes these also provide some evidence of achievement. In design and technology, intermediate products might be in the form of a written account, a picture representing a need or problem, a design sketch or a procedural plan. A portfolio of work can be collected, such as the written accounts, pictures, print outs of different stages in an activity and sketches of the end product.

With information technology, samples of work – word processing, pictures or design layouts, sequences and instructions for control – could also be stored in the portfolio. Examples of the children's work should be collected over time and therefore it is often useful for the teacher to add notes to the back of the work to make it meaningful at a later date.

Setting specific tasks

If assessment of a particular skill or concept is required, then a specific task can be used. The teacher sets a problem to solve or a written task to be completed. The latter is well suited for assessing knowledge and understanding. For example, which tools would they use on particular materials? Why would they use these tools? Why is the order of the instructions to control a robot important? What will happen if the sequence is rearranged?

Assessment tasks which are useful for this purpose include:
• *Cloze tests:* clozure means filling in the gap. Children can be given sentences or

passages in which key words are omitted
and they are asked to complete them with
the appropriate words or phrases.
• *Concept maps:* concept mapping is a
useful way of finding out what ideas
children have before they begin a task and
what new ideas they have developed as a
result of the experience.

Children are given groups of words
which they connect according to what they
already know or understand. It is useful to
ask the children to join pairs of words
together to make a sentence which
describes what they know or understand
about them. This can be done orally or in
written form, and with younger children the
words can be presented as pictures.
• *Comprehension exercises:* written or taped
questions can be asked of the children in
order to monitor their skills, knowledge and
understanding.
• *Crosswords:* familiarity with vocabulary,
terms, names of tools and so on can be
checked by giving the children a crossword
to complete. Either the children use the
clues to complete the grid, or they can be

given the completed grid and asked to write
the clues for another child in the class.
• *Extended writing:* ask the children to
describe what they have been doing in their
own way, placing no constraints on the
structure or format of the writing so the
style is free.
• *Multiple-choice questionnaires:* primary
children enjoy this kind of task. Present
them with questions which have four or
five alternative answers, only one of which
is correct. This method can be used to
check tools and materials being used and
also technological strategies being
employed. It is really a test of recognition,
rather than unaided recall and sometimes
guessing can occur.
• *Word and picture matching:* with younger
children this technique can be used to
check how they would choose tools and
materials for specific tasks.
• *Word-searches:* this is an interesting way
of monitoring vocabulary familiarity.

Examples of some of these are given in
Figures 6.4 to 6.8.

Concept: the properties of a material determine the tools used to work with it.

What to do

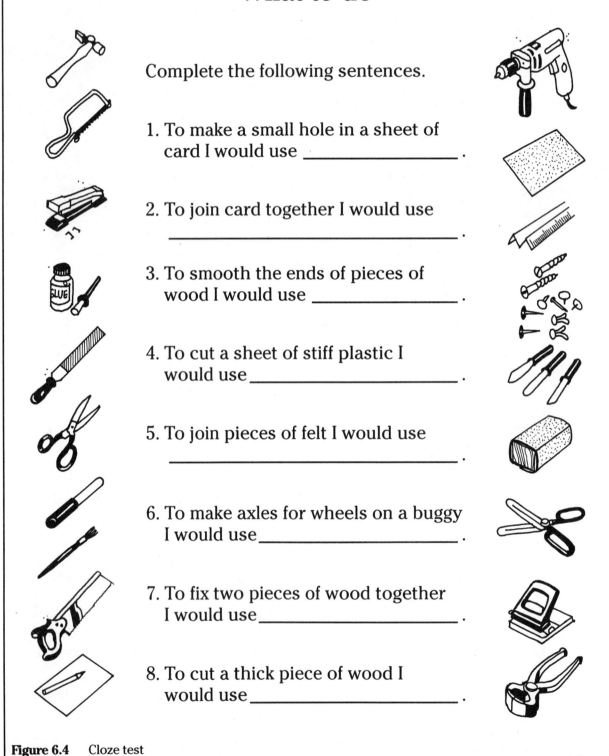

Complete the following sentences.

1. To make a small hole in a sheet of card I would use _____.

2. To join card together I would use _____.

3. To smooth the ends of pieces of wood I would use _____.

4. To cut a sheet of stiff plastic I would use _____.

5. To join pieces of felt I would use _____.

6. To make axles for wheels on a buggy I would use _____.

7. To fix two pieces of wood together I would use _____.

8. To cut a thick piece of wood I would use _____.

Figure 6.4   Cloze test

Design and technology: concept mapping

Name: _Andrew Smith_   **Date:** _February_   **Class:** _Year 6_

Words to link:

energy ✓   gravity ✓   friction ✓   axle ✓

force ✓   wheels ✓   spring ✓   battery ✓

move ✓   elastic band ✓

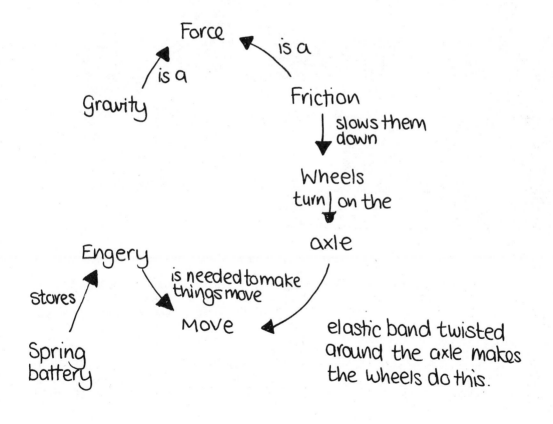

Figure 6.5

Tools and materials: crossword

Across:

1. A white powder from France? (7,2,5)
7. Fine, soft powder made by grinding wheat or corn. (5)
8. Fit one of 6 down then hold this firmly and turn the handle to make holes. (4,5)
10. Like 9 down — but this one is for juniors! (7)
12. Triangles of this can be stuck on to frameworks for strength. (4)
13. The wooden block you fix over the end of the table to hold wood firmly for cutting. (5,4)
15. Sounds nice, but it's jaws will grip and cause pain! (4)
16. Tool used to drive a nail into a block of wood. (6)

Down:

2. A rough sheet used to smooth wood. (4,5)
3. The rod which connects wheels. (4)
4. A tool which twists a screw into place. (11)
5. Thin yarn, used in sewing. (6)
6. Pencil-like metal rods which fix into 8 across to make holes. (4)
9. Tool with teeth for cutting wood. (3)
11. Oak, pine and jelutong are all types of _____ . (4)
14. A drill or a punch can make one of these. (4)

Answers

Across
1. Plaster of Paris; 7. Flour;
8. Hand drill; 10. Hack-saw;
12. Card; 13. Bench hook;
15. Vice; 16. Hammer.

Down
2. Sandpaper; 3. Axle;
4. Screwdriver; 5. Thread;
6. Bits; 9. Saw; 11. Wood;
14. Hole.

Figure 6.6

Concept: the properties of a material determine the tools used when working with it.

What to do

Draw a line from each tool to *one* material on which you would use the tool.
The first one has been done for you.

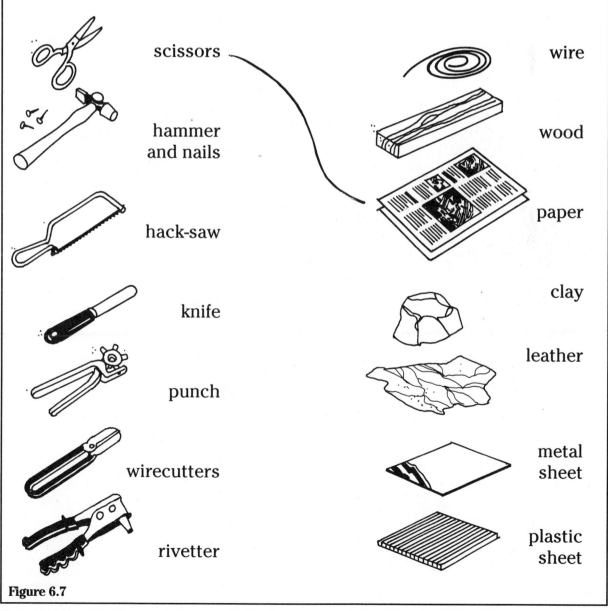

scissors — paper

hammer and nails

hack-saw

knife

punch

wirecutters

rivetter

wire

wood

paper

clay

leather

metal sheet

plastic sheet

Figure 6.7

Tools and materials: word-search

```
H A J P R O T R A C T O R B D
P A N S A W B O A Z H R K U T
M S M E T A L R B M A N M R H
R S U M S A D S V Y C S C O R
G M Q S E C R A F T K N I F E
N T V C L R I Y S N S O Z E A
I Z I R M Y L Q K J A R T R D
R D P E C O L D I U W H E B Q
T A A W U T B U S I C O N A N
S A N D P A P E R N E F O X L
I K C R V X C A U A N T N D V
F E R I W L O P L I E R S A W
O R I V E T S H E L P R A N T
G L U E G U N Q R C V S W H Y
G B E R E L N S C I S S O R S
```

Can you find these words?

- card
- craftknife
- drill
- glue gun
- hacksaw
- hammer
- metal
- nail
- pliers
- protractor
- punch
- rivet
- sandpaper
- scissors
- screwdriver
- string
- tenon saw
- thread
- wire
- wood

Figure 6.8

Involving children in their own assessment

If children are to become independent learners, taking responsibility for their own learning, then they should be allowed to take some responsibility for their own assessment by evaluating their learning. This needs to be developed slowly and with care. If children are encouraged to believe that their opinions and reasons matter, then they will put this belief to good use when participating in self-assessment. A starting point for this is a technology plan-do-review sheet (see Figure 6.9).

Children of all ages are capable of completing these sheets and usually do so with a remarkable degree of honesty and self-criticism. With older children, asking them to keep a diary or learning log is another way to encourage them to reflect upon what they are doing, how they feel about the experiences and how they would like to change or improve things.

Initially, questions can be used to aid their self-evaluation. For example,
• What did I actually do?
• What did I learn?
• Did I enjoy what I did?
• If I was able to do it again, what would I do?
• What am I going to do now?

Such questions can also be asked by the teacher in order to analyse the events and how effective they were. For example,
• What did the children actually do?
• What skills, knowledge and understanding, and personal qualities were they developing?
• How worthwhile was it?
• What do I intend to do next?

When should assessment take place?

Planning technology experiences for a class is relatively easy (see Chapters Nine and Eleven). Assessing the progress of the children is a very different matter. In a busy, full classroom, with many other demands on the teacher, finding the time is often difficult. In addition, the nature of technological activities is such that children may be working in groups, perhaps planning and making or using a computer. Identifying a child's contribution in a group effort and identifying his or her particular skills and understanding presents difficulties. At the same time, separate skills, ideas and personal qualities can be developed and fostered through specific activities but their application is often through more open, general activities at a later stage in a child's education.

If assessment was left to the end of a key stage or even to the end of each academic year, it would be an impossible task. It is more practical to assess a different group every few weeks so that by the end of a term every group will have been assessed at least once.

My name is _____

The people in my group were

_____

_____

We had to

My idea was

The part I did was

I used

I think

My teacher thinks

Figure 6.9

Recording

Should progress in technology be recorded?

Schools need to keep some sort of record of each child's progress for several reasons. First, so much happens in a classroom that it is not possible for a teacher to remember everything that each child achieved. Second, bringing together information collected informally at different times and from different kinds of experience or activity allows a teacher to see patterns in a pupil's progress. It also allows areas of strength or weakness to be seen. Third, records aid communication with pupils about their progress, with other teachers and with parents.

This suggests that there should be an efficient and informative system of record keeping. However, it must be remembered that record keeping is not an end in itself, but is merely a stage in the cycle of evaluating achievement.

Ideally, formal records should:
• provide only that information which is needed;
• be neither arduous nor time-consuming to maintain;
• be capable of contributing to planning and decision-making at all levels;
• show progress and continuity in experiences;
• be consistent throughout the school;
• be regularly reviewed and updated.
   Records will need to indicate:
• the activities or experiences offered to pupils;
• the end products of the technological activities;
• the children's reactions to the experiences or activities. Did they find them interesting? Were they matched to needs and abilities? Did they develop skills, knowledge and understanding, positive attitudes and personal qualities? In what contexts were the activities encountered? What practical difficulties did the children have? What intellectual difficulties did the children have? What National Curriculum statements of attainment were achieved?

What types of record can be made?

Formative or diagnostic day-to-day records

Activity lists: teachers need to record the general experiences and activities in technology which children have undertaken, identifying topics or themes followed, projects developed and workcards or task sheets completed. These records reflect progression and continuity in experience through the class and school.

Free comments: the observation notes can take on this role, in that teachers jot comments in a notebook or diary on individual children as they work. These should reflect how the children are reacting to technological experiences, and should also make use of the children's own comments and evaluations. Short entries made regularly build into a detailed picture of the whole child and serve as an *aide-mémoire.*

Criterion-based check-lists: teachers may also devise a list of suitable descriptors or questions based on the criteria mentioned earlier. Completing these check-lists builds a profile of the children's development of skills, knowledge and understanding and personal qualities.

Ratings or grades: these are similar to the check-lists described above, but the descriptors or criteria are graded in steps, for example, 1 to 5, A to E, or good/satisfactory/poor.

Implicit in such a grading or rating system is the notion of the 'average' child, and so the system builds into it comparisons of children around an expected normal or average behaviour.

Test scores: when knowledge or content is being assessed and a mark is awarded, the performance scores can be recorded. For example, the score obtained by a child completing a word-picture matching task, reflecting his or her ability to match tools to materials, could be recorded in this way. Copies of such tests should be retained in the child's portfolio along with other records.

Summative records

The final step is to turn the information collected in these ways into a summative record of the child's overall progress and achievement. By necessity, this needs to be as informative but economical as possible. Recording wheels, as shown in Figures 6.10 to 6.14 are one way to do this. With the recording wheel the teacher can see at a glance what National Curriculum-defined processes, skills, knowledge and understanding have been achieved, and the areas of strength and weakness. The compact format of the wheels is also useful for reporting, whether to other teachers or to parents.

Reviewing and improving records

The form and content of records must be regularly reviewed and, if necessary, revised in order to match current approaches and ideas. This is very much a whole-school task, since if all teachers are to use the records they must also be involved in their planning and design.

Recording wheel:
AT1: Identifying needs and opportunities

Name: _____ Date of birth: _____

Reception	Year 1	Year 2	Year 3	Year 4	Year 5	Year 6
4-5	5-6	6-7	7-8	8-9	9-10	10-11

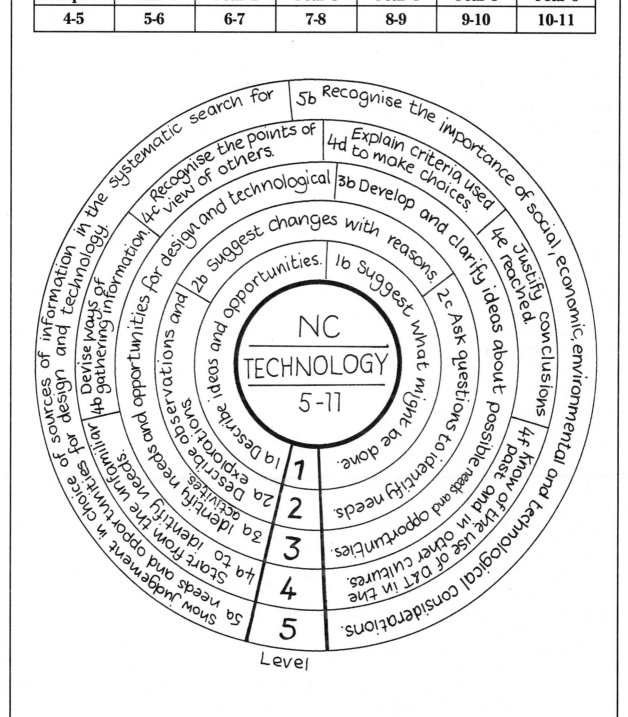

Figure 6.10

Recording wheel:
AT2: Generating a
design

Name: _____ **Date of birth:** _____

Reception	Year 1	Year 2	Year 3	Year 4	Year 5	Year 6
4-5	5-6	6-7	7-8	8-9	9-10	10-11

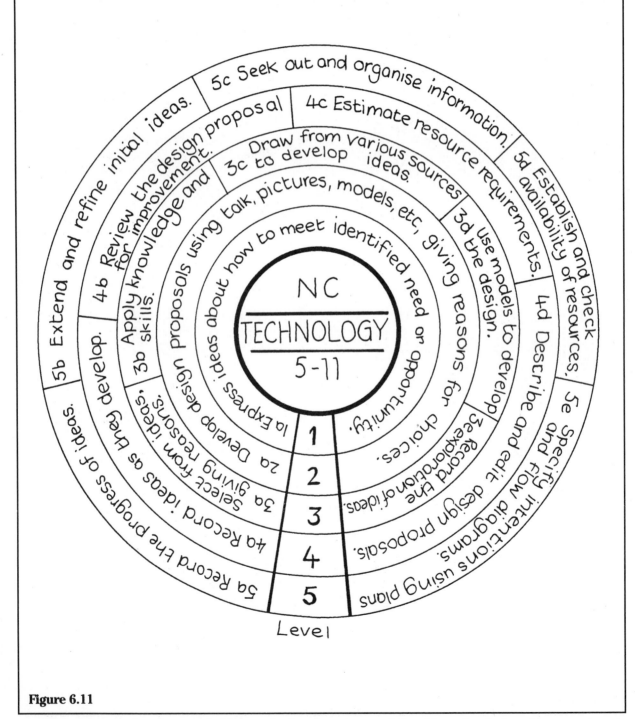

Figure 6.11

Recording wheel:
AT3: Planning and making

Name: _____ Date of birth: _____

Reception	Year 1	Year 2	Year 3	Year 4	Year 5	Year 6
4-5	5-6	6-7	7-8	8-9	9-10	10-11

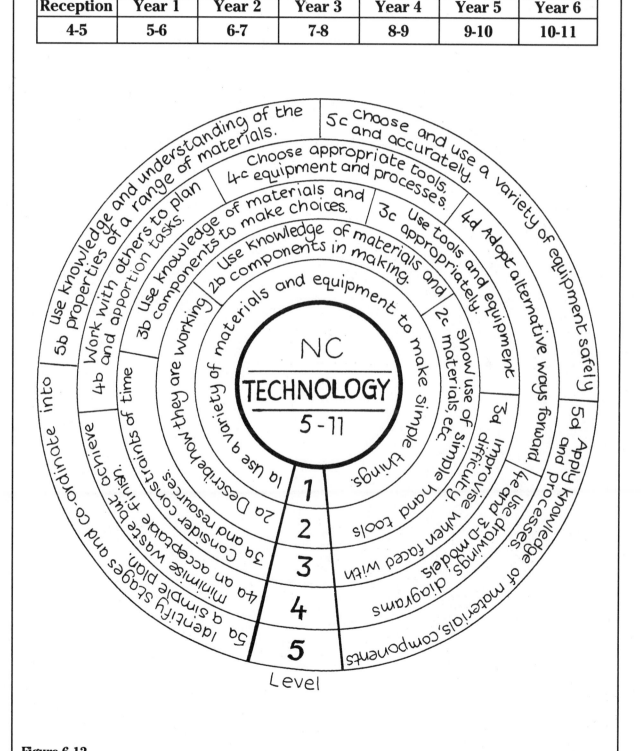

Figure 6.12

Recording wheel:
AT4: Evaluating

Name: _____ Date of birth: _____

Reception	Year 1	Year 2	Year 3	Year 4	Year 5	Year 6
4-5	5-6	6-7	7-8	8-9	9-10	10-11

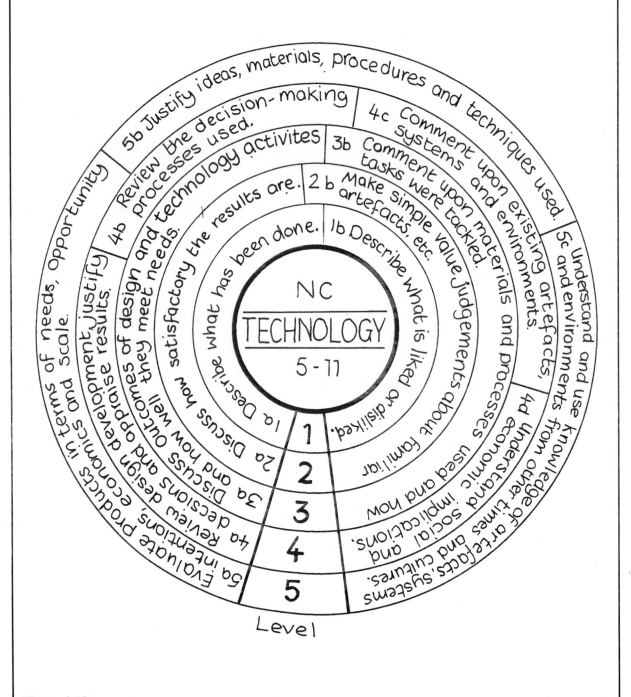

Figure 6.13

Recording wheel:
AT5: Information technology

Name: _____ Date of birth: _____

Reception	Year 1	Year 2	Year 3	Year 4	Year 5	Year 6
4-5	5-6	6-7	7-8	8-9	9-10	10-11

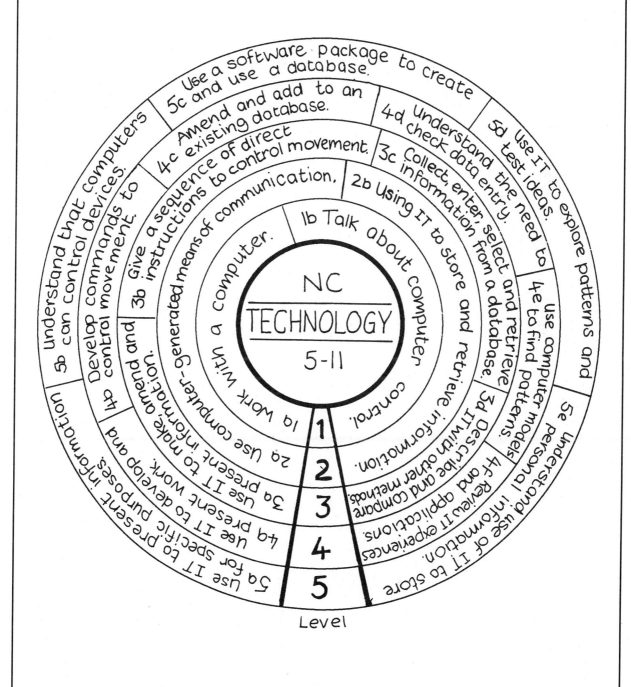

Figure 6.14

Chapter seven
Policy into practice

Technology in the National Curriculum makes it clear that the headteacher should: **'consider with his or her staff whether existing schemes of work adequately cover the attainment targets and programmes of study, or, whether the schemes of work need modifying'** *DES Circular 3/90.*

This is no light task since, until very recently, technology as defined by the National Curriculum was rarely taught in its fullest sense in primary schools. Where it existed at all, it was likely to be subsumed by art and craft or arose out of problem solving in science. This is not, of course, unreasonable, since technology as a process has strands which permeate many areas of the primary curriculum. The task now facing school staff is how to untangle these strands and strengthen them, so that technology can stand in its own right as an

important area of experience for young children. *Technology in the National Curriculum* provides us with a framework for developing the technological capabilities of children. Resource books for teachers, such as *Bright Ideas: Design and Technology* (Scholastic, 1990), offer technological activities for the primary classroom and suggest appropriate activities which complement common teaching topics and themes. What remains is for the staff, led by the headteacher (perhaps with some guidance from an advisory teacher for technology or someone from the local higher education institution) to construct a realistic policy for technology education. This chapter offers one possible programme which can be followed over the period of a school year to develop a policy for technology education.

A PROGRAMME FOR DEVELOPING A POLICY

	Who is involved?	How are they involved?	What is the end product?
TERM 3	All teaching staff plus outside experts	(a) Orienting (b) Focusing (c) Familiarising	**Policy Statement:** succinct summary of nature, purpose and management of Technology throughout the school
TERM 2	All teaching staff with help from technology coordinator or LEA advisory teacher	(d) Organising	**School Programme:** written statement of broad experiences planned for children over specified time span (eg Primary Phase, Key Stage); schemes of work for each Key Stage
	Individual teachers	(e) Planning	**Planning webs and lesson plans:** specific objectives, methods, organisational strategies, resource needs and cross-curricular links
TERM 1	Individual teachers	(f) Implementing (g) Evaluating	**Class activities Assessment:** of children's progress and achievement **Record keeping:** of work planned, which experiences were offered, which completed, what was achieved
	All teaching staff		**Appraisal:** of the programme for fine tuning

Figure 7.1

A programme for developing a policy

The school's policy for technology should have the following elements:
- a policy statement;
- a school programme of work;
- schemes of work;
- topic/theme forecasts;
- lesson plans;
- evaluation formats.

Of course, the policy developed should be in accord with the school's general philosophy or rationale, the methods of teaching used, approaches and organisation, space, time and resources and the specialist support that is available. There is always a danger with policy documents that, once written, they become cast in concrete. Since it is a policy developed by the whole staff for that staff, it should also be a policy which evolves and changes over time as needs change. Policy documents should be reviewed regularly and altered or updated as required.

The policy statement

The development of a policy statement is very much a whole staff exercise. The statement should identify the nature, purpose and management of technology throughout the school. Through the development of a policy statement all teachers should come to a common understanding of what technology is and should reach broad agreement on how the aims and objectives in technology education can best be achieved in their school. The policy statement must be general enough to allow individual teachers freedom and flexibility to use their own strengths and interests. It must also be specific enough to provide structure for progression and continuity and support for new or inexperienced teachers of technology.

In order to develop the policy statement, staff will need to go through a series of stages or processes: orienting, focusing and familiarising.

- *Orienting* provides opportunities for teachers to think through and express their own understanding of what technology means to them.
- *Focusing* enables perceptions and understanding to be clarified in the light of current educational views, particularly with reference to the National Curriculum. The key issues and principles can be highlighted and explored.
- *Familiarising* involves the staff in practical workshops to experience for themselves the reality of design and technology and information technology. It is only by being involved in the process ourselves that we begin to understand what is needed: time, resources, space, organisation and so on. Staff may also need extra in-service support to extend their own knowledge and understanding of key areas of science drawn upon in technology, such as forces and energy.

This is best done as a collaborative exercise, perhaps with the use of outside expertise, such as an advisory teacher for technology or a tutor from a local higher education institution. Some questions are provided which can be used to encourage discussion. Access to all the relevant documents is needed and there are also some useful video resources which can help in this stage. A visit to another school, where the staff have already gone through the process of developing a policy for technology, might also help.

Questions to ask during policy development
- *Orienting*

What is the staff's current understanding of technology?

What does technology mean to them?

How closely do their perceptions match the ideas in *Technology in the National Curriculum*?
- *Focusing*

What is the nature of technology?

Is technology a practical process or a body of knowledge?

Why include technology in the primary curriculum?

What is meant by problem solving as an approach in technology education?

What are the main aims of technology education?

• *Familiarising*

How much time do children need to do technology?

What skills will be used?

What attitudes will be fostered?

What knowledge and understanding will be drawn from other areas of the curriculum?

What resources will be needed?

• *Organising*

How do we put these ideas into practice?

Where do we start?

What contexts are relevant to our school?

What contexts are appropriate to different ages?

How much time will be spent on technology?

What resources do we already have?

What resources do we need to buy or collect?

How do we plan a school programme?

What cross-curricular topics or projects are covered in different classes?

What aspects of *Technology in the National Curriculum* can be developed through these topics?

Which skills and processes will be used and developed?

What knowledge and understanding will be drawn from other areas of experience?

Is any extra work needed to ensure breadth, balance, continuity and progression?

Can we plan a school scheme of work for technology in the light of the above?

• *Planning*

What topics or subject themes am I doing with my class?

How is technology going to develop within the framework of experiences which I am offering my children?

What will be my broad general aims for technology during this unit of work?

What will be my specific learning and behavioural objectives?

Have I provided for different needs and interests?

Have I taken relevant opportunities to link pupils' experiences across the curriculum and to real life?

What resources do I need?

How will the children be organised?

• *Implementing*

What will my role as a teacher be throughout the activity?

Do I know the entry/starting point for each child?

Do I know where I want each child to go?

How can I monitor the children as they work?

• *Evaluating*

How do I know when a child has achieved something?

How do I evaluate progress?

How do I record planning and progress?

Have I provided feedback to the children?

Have I appraised my own planning and organisation?

The school programme

The next stage is *organising*, in which the staff produce a written statement describing generally the work planned for the children over a substantial period of time. This could be for all seven years of the primary school. An alternative would be for staff teaching in each key stage to work together. The school programme for technology would need to develop in relation to whole-school planning, to cover the core and foundation areas of the National Curriculum and also to incorporate the various criteria for good practice already discussed.

Teachers would need to identify, for each key stage, the topics or themes which are likely to be developed and the sequence in which these will usually occur. If possible, where these topics are already established and in use, the schemes of work should be examined to identify opportunities for relating the programmes of study for technology to experiences elsewhere, with particular reference to skills to be

School programme for technology

		Autumn Term		Spring Term		Summer Term	
		1st half	2nd half	1st half	2nd half	1st half	2nd half
RECEPTION		HARVEST •Handling cutting, fixing range of materials (water, clay, junk, paper).	MYSELF •Name badges; •construction kit houses; •finger puppets	COLOUR AND LIGHT •Spinning colour disc on rod; •sugar mice, •sun hats.	PETS •Survey of class pets; •writing/draw; using overlay keyboard.	FOOD •Survey of favourite food; •making food for teddy bears' picnic; •foil moulds for jellies.	SEASHORE (visit) •Spade for sandpit; •mould for sandcastle; •story/draw using IT.
YEAR 1		WEATHER AND SEASONS •Using IT to make simple records and weather books; •shadow sticks.	SHOPPING (visit) •Shopping survey; •shopping lists; •food technology •carrier bag task	AIR AND WATER (Jack and Jill) •Kite •wishing well; •water carrier.	GROWING THINGS (Jack and the Beanstalk) •Plant holder; •labels for seed pots •windowsill cold frame.	FARMING (visit) (Old mac Donald) •Model farm; •gate with hinge and catch; •feed trays.	HOMES (Three little pigs) •Houses for three pigs; •home corner for classroom •dolls house.
YEAR 2		SCHOOL •Book mark; •pencil pot holder; •library corner •classroom routines.	CELEBRATIONS •Masks - decorations •menu for a party •puppet theatre.	TIME •Planning home routines; •sundials; •timers.	SOUND AND MUSIC •Making instruments; •electronic keyboards.	MOVING AROUND •Free-wheel buggy; •land yacht.	MINIBEASTS (visit to the park) •Designing and making homes for animals.
YEAR 3		ROMANS •structures/ towers and forts; •seige towers; •catapults •ballista.	WINTER •Dryer for gloves; •wellington sorters; •toys; •cards with moving parts.	FLOATING AND SINKING (who sank the boat?); •water transport •pontoon bridges.	BIRDS (RSPB talk) •Bird survey •bird with hinged wings; •bird table; •food/water dispenser.	PLANTS •compost frames; •mini-greenhouse; •plant waterer.	PLAYGROUND (visit) •Design adventure playground (co-operature).
YEAR 4		WEATHER •Weather records on database; •weather screen; •sensors and control; •news sheet.	CHANGES (Autumn fair fundraising events) •Refreshments •tent; doilies; •flag pole).	OURSELVES •Food survey •diet/menu; •pack lunches; •school tuck shop; •skeleton with moving parts.	LIGHT AND COLOUR •Lighthouse; •traffic lights; •fabric dyeing/ printing for cushion covers.	MATERIALS •clay; •thumb, coil slab and tossed pots and containers; •fabric •pencil case; •oven gloves.	CASTLES (visit) •Design and make a castle with draw bridge, portcullis, etc.
YEAR 5		AIR AND WATER •windmill •water-mill – using wind/ water power to lift load.	VICTORIANS •Fairs and fairground (roundabout; helter skelter; stalls).	COMMUNICATION •Traffic survey; •road surfaces; •spanning gaps; •wheel vehicles (powered).	ASTRONOMY •IT models and simulations (solar system; eclipses; constellations).	GEOLOGY •Rock sorters; •weighing machines; •tumbling machine for jewellery	POLLUTION (visit) •Litter survey; •device to pick up litter; •newspaper report.
YEAR 6		FORCES •Bridge challenges (various).	ELECTRICITY •Electronics control switches •burglar alarms; •vase challenge.	ENERGY •Powered vehicles (buggy, crane trucks etc);	TRANSPORT (visit to local railway station) •Designing and making a railway system (co-operative)	LEISURE •Recreation centre visit; •games; •rule books; •tickets; •notices.	WOODLAND (visit) •Nature trail design and guide; •tickets.

Figure 7.2

developed, knowledge and understanding to be drawn upon, and contexts or means by which this can be done. The programme will need to be structured to take into account time to be spent upon technology, resource needs and preceding and subsequent experiences. The end product will be a succinct statement of the technological experiences which will be offered to each class to meet National Curriculum requirements in a broad, balanced, relevant and progressive way. An example of such a programme is given in Figure 7.2.

Where topics or themes are new, then summative schemes of work must be developed. These identify in more detail a sequence of appropriate technological experiences which *could* be offered. There should also be suggestions for more open problems and challenges to reinforce and extend the work for those occasions when the children do not suggest their own.

Planning at the class level

The next stage is very much for the individual teacher. This is the process of detailed *forward planning*, which would involve taking the relevant section of the school programme and filling out the scheme of work for that particular unit. The starting point might be a planning web for the topic to cover a short period of time, such as a half term. The teacher would need to identify:
• general aims;

• specific objectives;
• contexts for activities;
• activities;
• resource needs;
• possible products/outcomes (allowing for the unexpected);
• attainment target coverage;
• assessment strategies.

This would be translated into action through the specific lesson plans, which would focus on selected objectives and activities, organisation and management, cross-curricular links, and individual needs and interests.

Class activities

The next stage is *implementation*, or putting this planning into action. The teacher's role is one of enabler. Having engineered the experiences, the teacher should encourage the children to work collaboratively, discuss their ideas, be independent and reflect upon their experiences. As they work, the teacher can observe and monitor their development, using a range of appropriate strategies. These observations will be used later to make judgements and decisions about each child's progress, provide feedback to the child and also to the teacher to aid future planning.

At this stage, there should be an opportunity for the whole staff (or key stage teams) to convene again to *evaluate* the programme and carry out fine tuning. The final step is full implementation.

Chapter eight

From syllabus to scheme of work: progression in technology

Design and technology capability

Given a syllabus and the requirement that design and technology capability is to develop, where do we start, and what do we do next? Some kind of structure is needed if activities are not to be haphazard, random events in a pupil's life, lacking coherence and leading nowhere. In a subject like history, for instance, there is a clearly-defined body of knowledge which has been taught to children for decades. It is possible (though not necessarily good practice) to assign the Romans to Year 4 and the Victorians to Year 6. Within this framework, children may learn about the processes of history at appropriate levels. However, *Technology in the National*

113

Curriculum does not prescribe a particular body of knowledge. How, then, can a progressive scheme of work be constructed when, for each year, what it will say is: *'invent things and solve problems'*?

The answer comes from a closer look at some inventing activities. Take, for instance, the case of the car cover. In storms it tends to blow off. The technologist's goal is to find some way of preventing this. The situation is readily appreciated and the solution is likely to be within the understanding of the layperson. On the other hand, consider the case of the automatic road barrier. It should never descend on a car but, on occasions, it does. The situation here may be readily appreciated but the solution might involve more sophisticated technology. However, in the case of the early Spitfire engine, which tended to cut out when the aircraft went into a dive, the situation and the solution are both likely to be more remote from many people's experience. The point is, that while all call for some inventing, the situations and things to be invented differ in their level of meaning and sophistication. Some situations are more familiar and more meaningful for us than others. Others need more knowledge, understanding, experience and know-how. The things to be invented can be ordered so that they are progressively more demanding – but what makes them more demanding?

Several factors affect how demanding, challenging or exacting a task is:
• the meaningfulness of the situation, context or activity;
• the kind of product required;
• the knowledge and understanding needed;
• the processes or strategies needed;
• the materials to be worked;
• the making skills needed.

These factors are not independent of one another; the material to be used, for instance, determines the making skills needed, and conversely, the skills needed may determine the materials chosen.

Contexts can vary in familiarity and meaningfulness. Activities with meaningful contexts facilitate integration of learning with existing knowledge. The home offers familiar contexts for designing and making. Industry is often less familiar to children so some of the processes, like chemical production for instance, will seem less meaningful and less relevant to younger children. The generally accepted direction of progression is from the more familiar to the less familiar context. The home, school and leisure are very rich sources of familiar contexts. Aspects of community life, business and industry can also provide meaningful situations for designing and making tasks, for example, the carnival, the shop and the garage. Stories, poems, pictures and television programmes known to be suitable for a particular group of children may also provide the contexts for technological tasks. The number of contexts available is limited only by the teacher's imagination and the children's age, ability and experience.

Whether products are *artefacts* like a buggy, pencil case or bird table; *systems* like a shopping list in the order of the shops to be visited, or a storage system for technology tools; or *environments* like a home for a pet guinea pig, or a nesting box, they can vary in complexity. Something to hold drinking water for birds might be a pot or some form of dispenser. Few would find the pot too demanding, but some could be defeated by the dispenser, even given knowledge and understanding of the individual parts. Relating a number of relatively simple but interdependent parts makes its own demand.

The *processes* (or *strategies*, as some prefer) of invention are essentially the same, whatever the task. As an activity, technology *is* the system of processes which gives rise to the technological products. Take a process out and it is like having a bicycle with no handlebars or pedals; the system goes nowhere in particular. However, this is not to say that the level of process needed is the same in all situations. This is what makes it possible to state levels of attainment in the four attainment targets of National Curriculum design and technology capability. For example, in **Generating a design (AT2)**, **'Draw a picture showing how they will make a . . .'** is at Level 2 while **'Draw up a plan for a . . .'** is at Level 5. Similarly, in **Planning and making (AT3)**, **'consider constraints of time and availability of resources in planning and making'** is at Level 3 while **'identify stages in making and co-ordinate these into a simple plan to ensure efficient use of time, materials and labour'** is at Level 5. The processes of technology are like a vase – cut them in half one way and you have no vase at all; cut them another way and you still have a vase, but a smaller one.

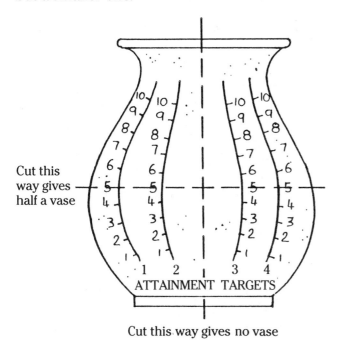

Cut this way gives half a vase

ATTAINMENT TARGETS

Cut this way gives no vase

Figure 8.1 Half a vase is half a vase or no vase at all: splitting technology vertically gives only fragments of technology; cutting across it still gives technology but at a different level of capability.

No design is conjured out of a vacuum. Underpinning it is *knowledge, understanding* and *experience*. Children should draw on their general experience and on the knowledge and skills acquired in other areas of the curriculum. Science, in particular, may contribute significantly to children's designing and making activities, especially regarding the properties of materials, energy, force, machines, stability, the strength of structures and shapes, electricity, and electronics. This may be

supplemented with information, knowledge and know-how from a range of other sources. Again, the situation or context is important. Where the knowledge and understanding it demands is outside the experience of the children, or beyond their comprehension, capacity or ability to find out for themselves, then it is inappropriate. As knowledge, understanding and research skills develop and awareness of the needs and beliefs of other people and cultures grows, so might the situations which underpin the activities. Knowledge and experience relate to the level of sophistication of the product which may be produced and which was described above.

The *materials* to be used will also be predetermined to some degree by the situation or context. Children who are to make hats for a school party are likely to use sheets of paper, plastic or fabric. They are unlikely to choose wood, clay, dough or sheet metal. This means that situations can be presented in the expectation that certain materials are likely to be used and that, over a period of time, pupils will work with a variety of construction materials, like clay, wood, plastics, metals, and with fabrics and food. It also means that tasks can be avoided which are likely to lead to the use of materials which are unsafe in inept hands, which involve materials not readily worked with the tools at hand or which are well beyond the present capabilities of the child. At the same time, when several different materials could be used to solve a problem, they might be restricted in size, shape or amount to alter the nature of the technology, the knowledge needed and the making skills used.

If an idea is to become a product, then *making skills* are needed. Some require little manipulative skill and use simple tools, like cutting paper with scissors and sticking the pieces with a adhesive stick. Others call for more control and concentration, like marking out the shapes to be cut, drilling, sawing and nailing. At the same time, children must learn which tools are best suited to particular materials, and how to

115

Situation or context	The kind of product	Knowledge and understanding	Processes or strategies	Materials and making skills
1	1	1	1	1
2	2	2	2	2
3				3
4				4
5				5
6				6
7		Level of demand increasing		7
.		↓	↓	.
.				.
	6	6	6	
	7	7	7	
	.	.	.	
	.	.	.	

Figure 8.2

join materials permanently and temporarily in more advanced ways. After sticking fabrics together, for instance, they might learn how to join them permanently with thread and temporarily with buttons. Having acquired the skill to shape material in a gross way, they need to move on and refine that skill, making it more controlled and precise.

In order to construct a progressive scheme of work, activities are devised with the appropriate level of demand in each of these factors. In theory, activities might be scored on a league table like that shown in Figure 8.2. The higher the score on each factor, the more demanding it would be. Conversely, a task with a low level of demand would be one which registers one on all factors. Put simply, an activity for very young children is likely to have a very familiar context and require little knowledge and understanding. Designing processes would be basic and skills might be limited to shaping materials by hand or with non-specialist tools.

As time passes, the activities (as a group) would widen the experience in such areas as structure, energy and control, and develop existing capabilities. In practice, the world is not obliged to provide a host of situations and activities which score at convenient and comparable levels on the chart. The task of replacing the figures in the chart with examples of activities, systems and environments is undertaken in Chapters Nine and Eleven.

Information technology capability

Information technology presents a similar problem: how to construct a progressive scheme of work. The first step is to look more closely at the nature of information technology. It has the character of a multi-purpose tool which serves at least four general functions. One function is to express information, thoughts and ideas in a form which allows them to be organised and developed and, when appropriate, presented and communicated to others. This might be through words, pictures or other computer-generated images and effects. Another function is to store and process information. This might involve collating, sorting, ordering and otherwise

116

processing information and informing the user about the outcome. A third function is that of modelling in which an aspect of the real world or some solution to a problem is simulated in the safe and relatively cheap environment provided by the computer. A fourth function is to provide automatic control, in which the computer monitors the progress of an event and maintains its direction along a predetermined path. These functions are not necessarily mutually exclusive – information might be handled and later communicated or used in control – and each one has applications which might affect the quality of people's lives.

Technology in the National Curriculum has described these strands of information technology capability as:
• developing ideas and communicating information;
• handling information;
• modelling;
• measurement and control;
• applications and effects.

Progression in information technology capability means, in effect, making progress in each of these strands. But this still leaves the problem of what is meant by 'doing harder information handling' or 'less demanding modelling'.

The National Curriculum identifies five aspects of progression for these functions:
• *task* complexity;
• *situation* familiarity;
• *skill* level;
• *dependency* level in using information technology;
• *software* sophistication.

Each of these affects the level of demand of a function and, in theory, a score sheet could be drawn up like that shown in Figure 8.3.

Some things remain unanswered; what is meant by task *complexity*, or an *advanced* skill, or *sophisticated* software, for instance? These need to be interpreted in the context of the functions of information technology, a task which is undertaken in Chapters Nine and Eleven.

Task complexity	Situation familiarity	Level of skill	Level of dependence	Sophistication of software
1	1	1	1	1
2	2	2	2	2
3				3
4				4
5				5
6				6
7		Level of demand increasing		7
.		⬇	⬇	.
.				.
		6	6	
		7	7	
		.	.	
		.	.	

Figure 8.3

117

Section two
National Curriculum technology

Chapter nine
A progression for Key Stage 1 technology

Design and technology

The example of a progression for Key Stage 1 design and technology which follows was constructed using the rationale described in Chapter Eight and takes into account the requirements of the National Curriculum .

The section **Artefacts, systems and environments** gives a sequence of technological products to illustrate those that suit this stage. These are only examples of activities and it is not necessary to attempt every one, or even any of those listed, if similar ones, better

suited to a topic or resources are available. Within each major division of product (artefact, system and environment) the progression begins with the least demanding tasks. Each product places demands on the pupil in terms of situation or context, knowledge and understanding, processes, materials and making skills. The subtitles indicate some of the demands made. However, the situation or story woven around an exercise can be used to tune the demand of an activity and the teacher can expect different levels of outcome from children of different capabilities. For instance, making a paperweight or a book mark could be activities at much the same level of demand, but working in different materials and with different tools. However, one could be tuned up to make a slightly greater level of demand by expecting more in, for instance, finishing or designing. For that purpose, progressions covering those aspects are also provided. There may be occasions when it is important to practise and consolidate what has been acquired and tasks should be designed accordingly. Pupils should also be encouraged to identify a need themselves and, whenever possible, design and make a product which satisfies that need. **Working with ideas** gives guidance on progression in that area.

Working with materials describes a progressive sequence of working skills within each of the areas: using tools, joining, and finishing. In addition, a sequence is described for working safely, and choosing materials.

Satisfying needs and addressing opportunities is concerned with the mental processes of invention: identifying needs, designing to satisfy a need, planning to realise a design, and evaluating outcomes. A progressive sequence is offered for each, and the knowledge and understanding a pupil may bring to the activities or develop through them is described. Similarly, some experiences which might precede the designing and making activities are suggested. **Working with ideas** describes stages and strategies in generating, developing and communicating ideas.

While these divisions reflect those of the National Curriculum programme of study, some readjustment was found useful in presenting the progression. **Artefacts, systems and environments** confines itself largely to the products of technology, **Working with materials** relates to the practical skills, and **Satisfying needs and addressing opportunities** to mental processes. The last division, **Working with ideas**, has been widened to include some discussion on ways of helping pupils generate ideas.

Using the progression

The examples of artefacts, systems and environments form a progression. With artefacts, for instance, it would be possible to begin with the activities like those at the top of the list for the younger children and reserve those at the bottom for the older children. This seems unnecessarily restrictive, for surely among the infinite range of possible products there must be some active artefacts which young children can make? Similarly, there will be occasions when older children's designing leads naturally to a passive, unjointed artefact. In other words, it seems better to avoid a hard and fast division according to age. Instead, we should think of progression as being the movement of the core of experiences through the list, as illustrated in Figure 9.1. At the same time, the core of experience will move through each aspect of each of the other areas of the progression.

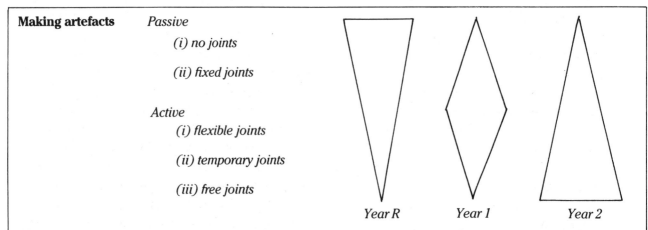

Figure 9.1   No kind of artefact, system or environment is the sole preserve of any one year group but the core of experience moves through the levels.

To illustrate, consider the topic 'Growing things'. In the reception class, 'Jack and the Beanstalk' might be used to set the scene for growing beans. The children could make something to help them plant their seeds (a dibber), something to hold the plant pot and, perhaps, a yoghurt pot waterer. They might be provided with cardboard, clay and plastic pots, and shape them without specialised tools. No joints would be needed, finishing could be by painting or covering with a self-adhesive material, and the children would be expected to tidy up after themselves. The teacher would discuss the need for these artefacts and would look for some recognition that these were potential solutions. In turn, the children would describe what they intended to do and would state whether their artefacts were satisfactory, perhaps on a 'plan-do-review' task evaluation sheet.

Year 1 pupils working on this topic might have a visit to a garden and collect some soil to grow cress seeds. The disadvantage of stony and lumpy soil would be apparent in attempting to fill margarine tubs. A need to remove the stones and lumps would be

discussed and suggestions for ideas stimulated by leading questions. How the ideas might solve the problem would be described by the children and they would select the most feasible one. A simple plan of action to make the solution (perhaps a cardboard box sieve and simple spade) would be made and executed. After using it, the children would have to comment on the performance of their artefact and identify a particular source of discontent (for example, the absence of handles).

Year 2 pupils working on the same topic might hear the story *Growing Vegetable Soup* by L. Ehlert (Gollancz). This might lead to some work in a school garden (for example, making a compost frame) or in the classroom (for example, making a window sill greenhouse). The children would need to clarify such things as how much compost is to go into the frame and then draw some possible designs. Choosing the one they feel is most likely to succeed, they might model it with a kit and set about making a full size version of it. The teacher would be at some pains to point out that, since everyone would see the frame, it should be carefully made and look attractive. Appropriate tools would need to be selected and used safely, tasks might be allocated to individuals and some improvisation might be necessary. Some immediate comments on what they would do differently next time could be elicited, but a further evaluation could take place after a few weeks of use. An account of the activity in writing and with drawings could be used as the basis of a display.

Procedure

It should now be apparent that a procedure for devising or selecting an activity could be as follows:
• Choose the kind of artefact, system or environment which suits the theme or topic in hand and which makes appropriate demands in terms of knowledge, understanding, materials and making skills. Be prepared to use or adapt a pupil's idea, especially where it arises from a need perceived by the child.
• Devise a situation, scenario or brief which fits in naturally with the current work and is likely to motivate pupils. When possible and appropriate, make it open-ended (couching it in such terms as, 'Invent something which will . . .').

• Use the appropriate parts of the progressions for **working with materials** (joining, finishing, working safely, using materials), **satisfying needs and addressing opportunities** (identifying needs, designing to satisfy a need, planning to realise a design, evaluating outcomes), and **working with ideas** (generating ideas, developing ideas, communicating ideas), clarify what is expected in these areas and, when appropriate, add conditions or constraints or devise a procedure which obliges the pupils to develop and extend their experience.

For example, in the reception class within the topic of 'caring', the need to care for the appearance of the classroom and personal belongings might be introduced. This could lead to the making of such artefacts as a pencil pot (no joints) or folder for work (permanent joints) using simple tools. The need for an attractive appearance could be emphasised and possibilities discussed.

In Year 1, within a topic on 'houses and homes' and after hearing the story of *The House that Jack Built* by W. Stobbs (Oxford University Press), the children might make a child-size house from a kit and a model house from a cardboard box, with the stipulation that the door on their model house must work (flexible joint).

In Year 2, within a topic on 'celebrations', the following scenario might be set: 'We are having a birthday/Christmas party but we have no decorations/hats/invitation cards/ puppets for entertainment. What are we going to do about it?'

As suggestions are made, a mixture of passive and active devices using various kinds of joints would be listed, discussed and allocated to appropriate groups for further development. All are reminded that it is a celebration so the decoration should be appropriate and amusing, and artefacts should be well-made. Each group is provided with further challenges relating to the assigned task; those making greetings cards, for instance, must include moving parts; those who make puppets might subsequently make a puppet theatre.

Artefacts, systems and environments

'In each key stage pupils should design and make artefacts (objects made by people); systems (sets of objects or activities which together perform a task); and environments (surroundings made, or developed, by people); in response to needs and opportunities identified by them' (*Technology in the National Curriculum,* **page 19).**

These activities are intended to illustrate an accumulation and development of experience in making artefacts, systems and environments. While examples of each are listed separately, any one may also be a representative of another group.

Beginning with the simple working of a range of materials by hand, with a spoon, or with scissors, the children learn to shape in other ways and to join materials. The processing of materials begins with drying and setting and is extended to supervised heating, when appropriate. The making of moulded structures, simple linear and flat shapes is widened to include three-dimensional models and two-dimensional frameworks. At the same time, simple hand-operated devices are introduced which also serve to illustrate single, mechanical processes. Designing environments begins with simple tasks which focus on satisfying one need (for example, tidiness, warmth, cleanliness). More demanding tasks require several complementary needs to be satisfied (for example, warmth and light; a light area, a dark area, place for food, and a place to hide). Some environments also serve to illustrate collections of complementary systems.

Construction kits make it possible to side-step some making difficulties such as joining, and thereby attempt activities at higher levels. Non-making activities may extend beyond the levels of demand of the making activities and prepare children for their future designing and making.

The examples below are neither prescriptive nor exhaustive and, in practice, may need to be tailored to suit a given situation.

Note that, for brevity, examples of actual products are listed. This is not to suggest that they should be presented as tasks in this form. Situations and contexts may be devised which are likely to lead to products like those listed. Compare, for instance, 'Make a paperweight' with 'Invent something to stop my papers blowing off the desk'. Each might serve a function but they offer different experiences.

Making artefacts
Passive

• *No joints*: a paperweight, a book mark, Christmas tree decorations, a desk tidy, a plant pot holder, a pencil pot, a back scratcher, a doily, a plant or seed dibber, foil moulds for jellies, sweetmeats for a party (for example, animals from fondant mix), something refreshing for a hot day for yourself/grandparents (for example, ice-cream from topping mix, orange fizz drink, fresh fruit salad).

•*Fixed joints*: a spade for the sand-pit, a brooch, badge or pendant, a mask, a finger puppet, a compost frame for the school garden.

Active

• *Flexible joints*: a model house with a door on a flexible hinge, a mobile, a bird with flexibly hinged wings, a castle with a flexibly hinged drawbridge, a hand puppet, a simple jack-in-the-box.

• *Temporary joints*: a pencil case with temporary fastening (button or tape).

• *Free joints*: a rod with spinnable colour disc (freely jointed), a draw-string bag for a physical education kit, greetings cards with

card push-up pieces, a crank-operated model wishing well, giant pick-up tongs, a free-wheel buggy, a land yacht, a puppet with freely-moving arms and legs.

Making systems

• *Single process*: a crank-operated model wishing well.

• *Several processes*: a kitchen.

• *Linear routines*: a sequential plan of action for tidying the classroom, a shopping list with items in the best order according to the shops that have to be visited.

Making environments

• *Few factors*: a teddy bear's picnic area, a book corner for the bedside table, a model sleeping place for a pet, a doll's house.

• *Several factors*: a home corner, a library corner for the classroom, a post office, a place to grow cress seeds, a home for a minibeast.

Some experiences which might precede designing and making tasks

• Examine and describe a variety of familiar structures (for example, playground equipment, physical education apparatus, household or classroom furniture), identify solid and hollow components, joints and the nature and method of joining.

• Identify and examine common joints (for example, zips, tapes, buttons and button-holes, hinges, pop-up picture joints).

• Examine toys with wheels and axles and recognise that freely turning joints are necessary for their action.

• Examine structures whose strength comes from bulk (for example, walls), number (for example, string, thread and wire flex), layers (card and papier mâché).

• Use kits to make models of objects around them such as walls, towers, bridges and houses.

• Look for regularity and pattern in the structure of objects (for example, the weave in cloth and wire gauze, brickwork and floor tiles).

124

• Examine structures whose strength comes from shape (for example, tubes and angle-iron shelves).

• Use toys, tools and common utensils which incorporate simple mechanisms such as levers, cranks, gears, pulleys and belt drives, and describe the action and interaction of the components (for example, a pedal car, rotary hand-whisk, rotary tin-opener, hose reel, bicycle, bicycle bell, mechanical clock and puppet).

• State the purpose of simple material systems, specify the action and the effect and locate the 'special' processing part (for example, rotary hand-whisk and wind-up toys). Identify the function of the parts of simple, collective material systems such as a bicycle, a house, a kitchen and a train set.

• Use devices which are powered in a variety of ways (for example, elastic-band propelled aeroplane or boat, battery-operated toy, pedal car, friction-drive car and torch). Visit a windmill or a watermill.

• Control things (for example, operate a simple mechanical puppet, use a switch to light a model house, set an oven to bake a potato and use a programmable toy).

• Examine familiar environments and find out what things are the same and what things are different about them (for example, the classroom, dining hall, staff room, cloakroom and library).

Some knowledge and understanding of concepts used in the tasks

Force

Forces causing movement, changing movement, and stopping movement: push, pull, twist and resultant changes in shape, bend, stretch, squash, sag. Observation of floating and sinking.

Energy

• *People power*: pushing, pulling, spinning, twisting, pedalling and blowing.

• *Other sources of power*: wind, gravity (falling and motion down inclines), free-wheeling. Storage of energy in such things as elastic bands, batteries and spinning wheels.

Electricity

• Simple circuits with bulbs, buzzers and motors.
• Conductors and insulators.
• The danger of the mains supply.

Shape and structure

• Strength in bulk and number.
• The strength of tubes.

Control

Making things do what we want: mechanical control with wheels, a push-pull rod, lever, crank or pulley.

Materials

See **Working with materials**.

Working with materials

'**Pupils should be taught to take reasonable care at all times for the safety of themselves and of others . . . At each key stage pupils should be given opportunities to work with a range of materials, including textiles, graphic media (such as paint, paper, photographs), construction materials (such as clay, wood, plastic, metal), and food'** *(Technology in the National Curriculum, page 19).*

Using tools

Using materials which have been prepared or pre-formed; tool-free kits; kits with simple tools (for example, large size keys or spanners); some common classroom or kitchen tools (safe scissors, grater or paper punch); simple workshop tools (junior hack-saw, hand drill, hammer, pliers and bodkin).

Joining

No joints; semi-permanent joints (stuck with adhesive); flexible joints (using adhesive tape), temporary joints (with buttons or tape); free joints (using paper-fasteners through card and wheels on axles); permanent joints (for example, by nailing); leading to an increasing competence in choosing an appropriate joint and ways of achieving it.

Finishing

Covering surfaces to alter the texture or to improve the appearance (crayon, paint, adhesive materials and attached materials); showing increasing control of the medium and any tool used; increasing care and precision, and developing aesthetic quality with time and practice. Choose a finish which will 'take' on the materials used. Give reasons for a particular choice of finish. Consideration of the need to treat surfaces prior to applying decoration or finishes (for example, smooth them with sandpaper and brush off loose dust).

Working safely

Store equipment after use; use tools with respect; use appropriate tool for a task; show awareness that activities might present dangers for others and show a concern for surroundings.

Choosing materials

Use those provided, such as paper, card, wood, clay, cooking foil, foodstuffs and fabric; select a suitable material by considering the main, relevant property; consider alternative materials with the main, relevant property and select from them on the basis of another relevant property (for example, appearance and durability).

Some experiences which might precede designing and making tasks

• Play games to match tools, tasks and materials with pictures and words, such as a picture of a knife, a picture of a loaf of bread and a card which says 'cut'.
• See tools being used expertly and the products made with them (perhaps in the school kitchen).
• Locate, examine and describe different joints used in the classroom (for example, door hinges). Dismantle and assemble simple artefacts with temporary joints.
• Examine and describe the finishes applied to walls, doors, tables and floor in the classroom. Suggest reasons for the choice of finish. Examine and describe the finish of a range of manufactured items like toys, floor coverings, pens and pencils, using sight and touch and realise that such things have been finished in a variety of ways.
• Discuss the need for safe working practices; create a safety poster for the technology corner; identify tools by their silhouettes drawn on a storage board; identify the most dangerous part of a tool and recognise when it is necessary to use safety spectacles or gloves.
• Assemble models (for example, a tower) in a range of materials (cotton reels, wooden blocks and matchboxes) and describe differences between them. Compare roofs, see a collection of roofing materials (slate, tile, felt and thatch) and recognise that different materials can have the same property and serve the same function. Compare coats in the same way.
• Recognise that the same material can

have several properties and so may serve several functions (cooking foil, for instance, might be used to make a simple switch for an electrical circuit because it conducts electricity; it might also be used as a mirror in a model lighthouse because it reflects light well). Play choosing games in which materials are selected for stated tasks, such as a soft fabric for dressing a doll.

Some knowledge and understanding of concepts used in the tasks

• Identify common materials used in the activities (metal, wood, clay, plastic, water, sand and air). Increasingly be able to discriminate between different examples of the same material (hard wood and soft wood; soft metal and hard metal). The existence of air and its compressibility (as in an inflated balloon). The ability of water to flow.
• Properties of materials detectable by the senses such as shape, colour, texture, heaviness, transparency and stickiness.
• Response of common materials to bending, twisting, pulling, stretching, squashing, impact, drilling, cutting, magnetism and electricity.

• Effect of water on common materials; waterproof and porous materials, soluble materials, paste making and papier mâché.
• Effect of heat and cold on materials (melting and hardening chocolate and drying cloth). Temporary and permanent changes (for instance, on baking yeast dough or on letting clay dry).
• Effect of time on materials: change, deterioration, aging, fading and decay.
• Natural and manufactured materials.
• The treatment of surfaces in simple ways.

Satisfying needs and addressing opportunities

'As pupils progress, they should be given more opportunities to identify their own tasks for activity, and should use their knowledge and skills to make products which are more complex, or satisfy more demanding needs' (*Technology in the National Curriculum,* **page 19**).

Identifying needs
Have needs and opportunities presented and explained; recognise needs and opportunities for designing and making with guidance in familiar, concrete situations (for example, when something goes wrong in the classroom) or meaningful, imaginary situations such as those described in a story; clarify such opportunities with guidance; identify and clarify opportunities with increasing independence.

Designing to satisfy a need
In connection with the above kinds of need; describe a need or problem to others, recognise a potential way of satisfying a need or a potential solution to a problem when presented with one. Discuss a problem with others, express own idea for satisfying a need, describe how an idea is likely to solve the problem, choose one idea and support that choice from two or three potential solutions to a problem. Take into account their knowledge, skills and the availability of materials in choosing an idea, develop a design orally, on paper or with a model perhaps using a construction kit.

Planning to realise a design
Collect together materials, describe what is being done, describe what will be done, order the actions to be done into a list, re-arrange a list of actions to avoid a subsequent making problem (such as

drilling a hole before assembling a framework), improvise when something unexpected arises, include in the plan of action the role of others in the group (for example, a division of labour to save time). (For making skills see **Working with materials**, page 126.)

Evaluating outcomes

Describe what has been achieved, state whether satisfied with the outcome, identify particular areas of success like appearance, function, consistency of operation, where there is dissatisfaction with a product identify the source and discuss the reason for it, state what could be done to improve the product (designing, planning and making stages), make simple modifications to improve the product's performance, notice problems caused by a product (it might, for instance, let water drip on to the floor), act on the lessons learned in subsequent activities.

Some experiences which might precede designing and making tasks

• Use the shop corner to clarify concepts such as 'buy and sell'. Find out the things which can be bought in different types of shops. Discuss the purpose of and need for shops (for example, food, clothing, furniture). Find out where goods come from and the function of lorries, trucks, delivery vans and goods trains.
• Discuss situations of need (for example, storage of toys, games or pencils in the classroom) and identify what is needed. Examine very familiar objects (a broom, for instance) and find out about aspects of designs such as length of handle, stiffness of bristle, angle of head.
• Carry out surveys of preferences among classmates and family (how do pupils spend playtime, which colour is preferred and so on). Compare results with those from other classes and other families. Examine and discuss pictures of homes, schools and shops from different parts of

the world. Examine and discuss styles of dress from different times and places (children's and adult's clothing).
• Make collections of packaging (biscuit packet wrappers or chocolate boxes) and note the variety in design. Collect and display carrier bags, note and discuss the purpose of logos and advertisements.
• Examine wallpaper designs, ornaments, toys, a variety of soft drinks, and state what is liked and disliked about them in terms of some aesthetic qualities. Compare preferences with those of a friend and identify the qualities of an object a friend likes or dislikes (for example, smell, feel or colour).
• Compare a range of artefacts which serve the same function (different types of spoons or pens) and test them to find the one which is best suited to its purpose. State what it is which makes it the best one for the job.
• Examine a manufactured item which has been found wanting (a mask where the holes for the eyes are badly placed). Clarify the cause of discontent and discuss what

could be done to correct the defect. Test the suggestion either directly or by making a more suitable item, if possible.

• Consider problems caused by the designing and making of others (such as the noise from a portable radio, new road or runway, the increased traffic near a new shopping centre) and weigh the disadvantages against the advantages.

Some knowledge and understanding of concepts used in the tasks

• Know that people want or need certain goods.
• Know that goods are bought, sold and advertised.
• Know that goods are designed, made and distributed.
• Know that other people have preferences which need to be considered in design.
• Know that preferences are influenced by values, cultures, beliefs and needs which may be different to their own.
• Know that there is a need to consider aesthetic qualities and know what some of these qualities are (for example, form, structure, colour, pattern, surface and scale).
• Know some examples of 'different kinds of art and design from the contemporary world and the past'.

Working with ideas

Generating ideas

To begin with, the initiative for developing and communicating ideas may depend on the teacher. It is useful to have a picture or some significant object present for children to refer to. For example, when setting the scene for the tiger in the cage problem drawn from the story of 'Sanjeev, the Tiger and the Fox' (see page 143), a painted cardboard box can serve as the cage. The problem is literally rendered tangible; the scale and nature of the objects involved are to be seen. As a first step, the children

could describe the problem to others; this is intended to focus their minds on the task and clarify the problem. Their thoughts may then be guided by leading questions and tentative suggestions which refer directly to the model and link it with ideas for solving the problem. Pupils should be encouraged to express and elaborate their ideas by reference to the model, using both words and gestures, and to test ideas directly on it. Later, a model or object might be omitted and the children have to find something suitable to work with.

The responsibility for generating ideas to solve simple problems in familiar contexts should progressively become the pupil's. The teacher's role in such situations becomes more one of pointing the way when necessary. 'Do you think we could lift the box with this hook and this rope?' might become 'We have a hook. What can we do with a hook?' Suggestions are reduced to pregnant hints which, in turn, are slimmed to mere seductive comments. The change should be gradual and smooth so that the pupil is challenged but not frustrated by insurmountable difficulties. Links are made with other relevant experiences the children have to draw on. They may, for instance, have been using a lever or pulley wheel in a science lesson, or else seen a working drawbridge on a visit to a castle. Bringing together these experiences and the problem increases the chance of solving it.

In the real world, the requisite experience or knowledge may be absent, incomplete or forgotten. In this case, the child has nothing relevant to bring to the problem and so another strategy is needed. By questioning, we need to elicit from the children an appropriate action: in the tiger problem this could be *lift*. The teacher now leads a brainstorming session on lifting things: How many ways? What could we use? or, if relevant materials are available, sends the children to look at books or pictures about lifting things.

Developing ideas

Strategies which might help a child to express an idea should be practised as soon as they can be used to effect. Initially, an idea might be described to an adult and later could be explained to other members of the group. Simple drawings also help to clarify thought and articulate an idea.

In the early stages, verbal accounts and drawings might include vague 'special bits' intended to do something that the child is uncertain about, perhaps using a pulley wheel or fulcrum for a lever. Unless these 'special bits' are addressed, they will often become the source of failure and frustration. At times, the mechanisms they call for may be such that the design is impractical at this stage. However, with the tiger's cage type of problem, simple ideas might be tried directly and overcome in the making. The pauses for thought that they cause can be turned to good effect by asking for suggestions from others so that a corporate solution results; the lesson being that several minds can sometimes be better than one. While it is obviously necessary to clarify the 'special bits' when *developing ideas*, it is usually better to be less

concerned with them when *generating ideas*. An over-concern with detail too early may stifle imagination so that no worthwhile ideas are produced at all.

Sometimes, it is particularly helpful to model a solution to a problem, especially when three-dimensional artefacts or moving parts are involved. Kits like Quadro include a small version for this purpose but simple models or mock-ups may be made with modelling wire, clay or card. Where scale is important, it helps to have a card cut-out of a person or, in the above example, a tiger.

In both developing and generating ideas, questions which clarify the need or problem should be suggested initially and subsequently encouraged. For example, the teacher might ask if it would help to know if the cage is heavy; later, a pupil might want to know how high a tiger is when it crawls. Some problems may require that data be collected by, for instance, interviewing classmates about their preferences, counting birds which come for breadcrumbs, or writing a questionnaire for the family to complete. This data may be stored, sorted and presented with the help of a computer.

Communicating ideas

To begin with, the teacher would introduce a variety of methods of communicating ideas and suggest those that are appropriate. Younger pupils might communicate with words supported by actions and refer directly to the objects concerned where vocabulary is still wanting. They could indicate the relevant parts of pictures to show what they want to make and then copy them. Later, they might complete a simple, pre-prepared designing sheet with a picture of their design and a pictorial list of the tools they will need.

Older children could be expected to supplement their drawings with a brief, written description of their solution. As their vocabulary and language skills improve, drawings could be labelled and lists of materials and tools included. When the children are working on tasks involving a sequence of sub-activities, they could also provide a list of those activities in the order that they would be done. Descriptions might also be recorded on tape.

Alternative ways of showing others their thoughts should be introduced. For example, a simple model in clay or wire or a picture drawn with the aid of a computer might be more effective than an ambiguous description (after all, a picture is supposed to be worth a thousand words). The need to communicate ideas is not confined to technology and there are obvious opportunities to develop communication skills in most areas of the curriculum (for example, in mathematics, the children might draw a plan of their bedroom with moveable cut-out rectangles for the furniture; in a topic on pets, they might draw a plan of a home for a pet).

While the teacher would continue to extend the pupil's repertoire of ways of communicating and develop their skills, the children would begin to take some responsibility for deciding which method would be the best one for the task in hand.

Information technology

The example of a progression for Key Stage 1 information technology which follows was constructed using the rationale outlined in Chapter Eight and takes into account the requirements of the National Curriculum.

For each of the strands of information technology capability, a general indication of demand made by task complexity, situation familiarity, skill level, degree of dependence expected, and level of software sophistication is given. In order to clarify the levels of demand and to illustrate a progression, short sequences of activities are offered. It should be emphasised that these are illustrative, not prescriptive.

Using the progression

Resources vary from school to school and class to class so, while the activities listed will often be feasible, others may be devised and fitted in at appropriate points. To this end, the National Curriculum recommends that a chart of available software be compiled to show how and when it is to be deployed (Figure 9.2).

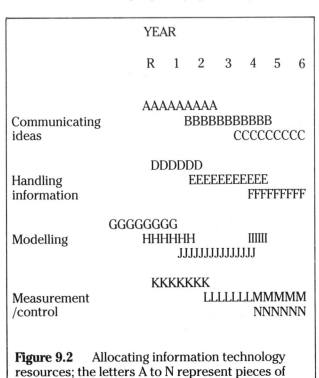

Figure 9.2 Allocating information technology resources; the letters A to N represent pieces of software.

Procedure

• For a given topic or theme, list the activities and experiences in it relating to design and technology and other areas of the curriculum.

• From the list, identify opportunities to develop particular strands of information technology capability.

• Structure those opportunities so appropriate activities like those in the progression for which software is available are integrated with them.

• Check for or devise opportunities to develop other aspects of information technology awareness, as described in the **Applications and effects** strand (page 138) and by activities which do not involve direct use of the computer. (When the hardware is in use with one group, it may be possible to pursue alternative aspects with other groups of children).

For example, for the topic on growing things, the reception class might make labels for their pots of seeds with the help of the teacher. Year 1, on their visit to a garden might find out how the temperature in the greenhouse is controlled using windows. On their return and helped by the teacher, they could then describe a garden visit in two or three simple sentences and illustrate the account with a picture chosen from a bank of illustrations offered by the software. They might also use a garden adventure game. Year 2 might keep a simple class diary of their work in the garden and maintain a record of the weather.

In places, the National Curriculum programme of study implies that children will set the controls of electrical equipment which operates from the mains supply (for example, tape recorder, microwave oven).

The teacher needs to consider if and under what conditions such tasks are appropriate, bearing in mind the safety of the children and the need for them to respect the mains electrical supply.

Developing ideas and communicating information

Information technology is described as a medium for enhancing and extending the experiences of writing, drawing and painting. The keyboard is not intended to replace other ways of producing text, illustration and self-expression. It is to be seen as one means of doing so having, like the other means, its own advantages and limitations.

Task, situation, skill, dependence and software

The pupil begins with simple, short tasks, recording brief pieces of information relating to familiar situations drawn from immediate events and needs relating to home, school and the child. Initially, this could require an emanuensis – someone to type in the information – or a simplified keyboard, like an overlay. Later, the pupil would be guided and helped to use a fuller, more usual keyboard. The software will tend to control and structure the decisions that are needed and limit the choice to a manageable size.

Activities

• Making name labels for their work, labels for trays, pots, doors, displays, items in the shop or home corner. 'This book belongs to . . .' labels.
• Making headed paper for selected pieces of work, such as an A4 blank sheet with the pupil's name and class at the top for use in art or technology.
• Making structured sheets giving name, story title followed by a space with ruled lines, picture caption for example.
• Select computer-generated pictures, symbols, and words or phrases to describe a real or imaginary event (a collection of pictures to show what games were played, words relating to bonfire night, items for a shopping bag, sounds from a mouse, 'Old Macdonald had a farm' – words by teacher, sounds and pictures by pupils).

• Write two or three statements about a real event using a word processing package for young children and illustrate it with a picture taken from a bank of illustrations ('How I made my . . .', 'The pond', 'The weather today is . . .').

• Write a few sentences of continuous prose to form a narrative of some imaginary event or some classroom experience linked to topic or theme using a word-processing package for young children and illustrate it with a picture taken from a bank of illustrations or using a simple draw facility. Correct work (for example, delete, erase).

• Organise, amend and modify work by adding, inserting and altering information already entered (insert a new or omitted idea in an appropriate place in a story, draft a description of a castle and later amend it after being checked by the teacher).

• Maintain a class diary, storing the day's events and later retrieving them for daily additions (weather, life histories of a tree in the playground, a stick insect, or a pet).

• Construct a tune, play it, and modify it, store it and replay it using a tape recorder; use a simple electronic keyboard.

Handling information

Information handling refers to the computer's ability to store, sort, organise and otherwise process information. The ability to manipulate information is important, but so is asking the right questions and knowing if they have been answered. By taking some of the burden of manipulation, the computer frees the pupil to practise and develop such capabilities.

Task, situation, skill, dependence and software

With advice and guidance, the pupils begin with small scale tasks in which they record simple categories of data relating to familiar things and situations with pencil and paper (for example, floaters and sinkers, bird visitors, pets, favourite toys). The software could ask for the information which might be entered by an emanuensis or with a simplified keyboard, part of a keyboard, or from a menu.

Activities

• Sorting, grouping, and classifying objects according to simple properties detected directly by the senses (colour, feel and so on). Counting the numbers in the groups and recording the data with simple pictures or pictograms in some organised form.

• Counting occurrences (number of birds visiting the bird table) and recording the result using computer-generated pictograms or the numerical keys on a teacher-prepared list.

Modelling

The computer can be used to model or simulate events in the real or in an imaginary world.

Task, situation, skill, dependence and software

Pupils interact with computer simulations of familiar and meaningful situations using, for instance, a simplified keyboard, a menu, mouse or joystick, and observe the outcome of their actions. While the software itself may be sophisticated, it places relatively low demands on the child as far as the complexity of the choices offered are concerned.

Activities

• Use simple games which simulate activities in the real world, such as blow football.
• Use simple computer simulation games and activities which have one clearly defined objective, for instance sports simulations.
• Use simple, low technology adventure games (branching books for example).
• Use simple adventure games based in familiar environments linked to topics and themes (a garden, a street, a wood). Construct a picture, model, or map of the environment they were in.

Measurement and control

Computers do not have to be mere passive receivers of information from a keyboard. With the help of a variety of sensors they can automatically collect information about the real world, record and process it, and deliver the results on demand. Neither need they only have an inwards flow of information. The computer can send instructions out to devices to make them perform complex operations. Put the two together and the computer may be used to measure, gauge or monitor a situation and respond to it with appropriate instructions.

• Recording hair or eye colour against a pre-prepared list of the pupils in the class.
• Responding to questions asked by the computer (How many children are there with blue eyes?) and using the numerical keys to answer.
• Recording information about daily events (Is it sunny today? [Write YES or NO] How many children are in the class today? How many children walked to school?)
• With a suitable piece of software, record, store, and retrieve data relating to daily or weekly events, updating it, as needed. Check and correct entries.
• Describe and discuss the outcome of any automatic computer processing (It has been sunny for . . . days this week; . . . children stayed for dinner this week).

Task, situation, skill, dependence and software

The pupil should experience the use of electronic devices in measurement and control in everyday life and in the classroom. Their tasks should involve using information technology to measure some meaningful aspects of the environment with guidance. The software would reduce the level of demand so that decision-points are clear to the child, choices simple and few, and keyboard skill relatively low.

Activities

• Control toys in various simple ways such as by using switches and brakes.
• Count the places in the school where devices are switched on and off manually.
• Observe how a television, radio or tape recorder is controlled (on/off switch, volume control). Identify the action and the response (push on a button and the doorbell rings; put on the brake and the bicycle slows down).

• Observe how a microwave oven is controlled (on/off, temperature and time).
• Observe the action of a thermostat in controlling a kettle, iron and the temperature of a room. Describe what will happen when a thermostat is altered to a new setting.
• Identify other instances of automatic control in the home and school, such as washing machine, drier, video-recorder and time switch.
• Try control at a distance (an electric toy operated through wires or a radio controlled car).
• Play games with defined moves (draughts and chess).
• Play pencil and paper games with 'programmed' moves, for instance battleships.
• Give instructions to a friend who will behave like a robot.
• Plan a sequence of instructions to conduct a friend through a maze.
• Give instructions to a programmable toy.
• Control the movement of a screen turtle.

Applications and effects

Applications of information technology are widespread, diverse and of various degrees of sophistication. In some cases, they have replaced earlier ways of doing things, in others they do more than was feasible before and they do new things. The effects are not always simple or obvious. As far as the quality of life is concerned, there may be gains and losses.

Task, situation, skill, dependence and software

Pupils should begin to appreciate the roles of information technology in the outside world and how their own experiences in the four preceding aspects relate to them. Beginning with relatively simple applications of information technology in familiar situations, pupils need to appreciate the number and variety. Whenever possible, the similarities between their own use of information technology and what they see in the outside world should be discussed.

Activities

• Draw attention to instances of the use of information technology at home (dimmer switch, telephone and washing machine), at school (tape recorder and digital clock) and on out-of-school visits (bar code readers at check-outs and cash dispensers).

• Provide 'hi-tech' models in the home and shop corners (a torch covered with red acetate film and attached by a cord to a table to serve as a bar code reader).

• Encourage pupils to talk about the applications of information technology they see, especially when they affect them directly (a computerised record system seen on a visit to the doctor or library; tickets which operate car park barriers or access to railway platforms; electronic central locking systems of vehicles; holiday booking at a travel agency).

• Compare the word processor with other ways of writing; consider the advantages and disadvantages (pencil and paper are simple and convenient, the word processor produces consistent and neat print).

• Compare pencil and paper and a simple database for recording and handling information.

Chapter ten
Starting points: Key Stage 1

Pictures, poems and stories

Pictures, poems, stories and television programmes are excellent vehicles for teaching children in many areas of the curriculum, and technology is no exception. They provide meaningful, concrete situations in which children learn and practise technology. The Programme of Study for Key Stage 1 states that pupils **'should . . . look at familiar things (such as pictures, poems, stories, television programmes) as starting points for some of their design and technological activities'** (*Technology in the National Curriculum*) but there is no pedagogical reason for confining the use of this strategy to this key stage alone. Appropriate pictures, poems and stories may be used to good effect in Key Stage 2 (or at any level, for that matter, for what else is the context of a design brief but a true story?). Often, the challenges offered by a story may be met at various levels of sophistication. In other words, the same story generates different solutions according to the experience, age and ability of the children.

Pictures

Pictures are commonly used with young children to develop vocabulary, language and communication skills, but they are common teaching devices in all areas of the curriculum. In science, for instance, a picture of washing being hung out to dry on a windy day might serve to draw children into a discussion about the elements of evaporation and the role of moving air. In history, an aerial view of a castle might be used to identify the main parts and describe their function. In English, a picture of a busy station with a family about to board a train might be a means of stimulating a child to produce an imaginative account of subsequent events. Pictures bring phenomena, events and other aspects of the world into the classroom when they are needed. They serve the same function in technology.

Some pictures might lend themselves to highlighting needs. For instance, a picture of a small child who has just issued from the end of the slide and landed with a painful bump on the concrete base could be used to point to the need for some sort of cushioning device, while a picture of a child enveloped in a hood and crossing the road on a rainy day might be used to indicate the need to see and be seen for the sake of safety. Each of these would lead to the designing and making of something to solve the problem. Others might be used to set the scene for activities which practise or extend technological knowledge. When using the picture of the castle in history, for example, it could lead conveniently to the designing and making of a model castle with a drawbridge operated by a winding handle. A picture might be used to enhance a story-telling session and, at the same time, provide the parameters of a problem to be solved. For example, Thomas the Tank Engine is rushing to his doom on a line that has been damaged by a storm. The children have to save him, perhaps with some sort of buffer placed across the bit of the line that has been washed away and tested with a toy train set. And, of course, pictures are useful for showing examples of artefacts, systems and environments. Illustrations of bridges show the strength of structures; a picture of a lock gate or a fairground might show levers, cogs and gears in action; a photograph of Antarctic exploration could show the importance of good environment design and the wise selection of materials.

Poems

Poems for children are often cleverly-packaged short stories which sometimes may be used as starting points for technology. Traditional or nursery rhymes are often taught to young children. Many are very old, have their origins in a pre-industrial society and tell us little about the devices with which we surround ourselves, today, but they may still point to needs and problems on which the children can sharpen their technological capabilities. For instance, 'Little Bo Peep' and 'Little Boy Blue' might, at first, seem to offer little more than a lesson in negligent livestock supervision, but they also point to an obvious need which children might try to solve. Some might suggest that the animals be restrained by a form of leash. When appropriate, the teacher would cavil and stretch their imagination further: 'But Bo Peep couldn't hold all her sheep on leashes; they would pull her wherever they wanted to go! What could we do about that?'

Inevitably, some rhymes are better starting points than others. For instance, the archetype of nursery rhymes, 'Jack and Jill' is very useful for introducing elementary work on hydraulics and practising technological capabilities: first, climbing a hill, drawing water, then struggling downhill with it is no easy or safe task. Given a bucket of water to carry, children soon identify the need (Attainment Target 1) for some means of transporting water easily and painlessly from the hill to their home. The first step is to think of some ideas, consider their feasibility and potential, and generate a design proposal (Attainment Target 2). The sophistication of the children's ideas depends on their age, ability and experience. Some might suggest

quality of the workmanship good enough; do the joints leak; does the water tank overflow; do the taps work? Fourth, would the solution be aesthetically acceptable: would an overhead ropeway be unsightly; should the water tank on the roof really be bright pink? Fifth, would it be environmentally friendly: does it spill so much water that what is at present a pleasant pasture will be rendered a stinking swamp? Sixth, would it be cost-effective: is it really necessary to use *gold* wire to fasten the pipes together?

Other rhymes provide opportunities for working in different ways and with different materials. Take, for instance 'There was an old woman who lived in a shoe': here is a chance for young children to identify needs and opportunities. What is the old woman's problem? Is it going to get better by itself? Might it get worse as the children grow? What could she do about it? This may lead to a group of ideas, probably of two kinds: adaptation of the shoe to make it more suited to her needs, and moving to a new home. The first kind should generate house extension designs while the second could lead to the design of a new home. Collections of house designs from sales offices are useful visual aids here and questions can focus upon what we want of a home, what we need, and the house as a system. The building of a house is hardly a feasible activity for the classroom, so the solution will have to be modelled, probably from cardboard boxes. Since the old woman could not really take possession and try it out, how well it suits her needs must, in the end, be a matter for the children's conjecture. The use of rhymes in teaching technology is described more fully in a short series of articles in *Questions*, May and June 1990.

While there are some rhymes with obvious potential, others like 'Hey diddle diddle', 'Old King Cole' and 'Georgie Porgy' seem more limited but, to some extent, the value of a poem or rhyme is determined by the teacher's ability to see whatever potential it has. Having said that and given that there are a number which lend

an open channel running from the well to the house, with a funnel at the well end. Others might prefer a chain of buckets on a rope, suspended from pulley blocks. Those with more experience might want to use a soap dispenser to pump water from the well through a tube to the kitchen sink, or better still, to a tank on the roof, so that water will literally be available on tap. Wells being what they are, planning and making (Attainment Target 3) in this case would have to be aimed at producing a working model which demonstrates the feasibility of the solution. Plastic pop-bottles, viscose tubing, plastic bendy straws, and clips as stop taps should cover most needs.

Having completed the model, it must be evaluated (Attainment Target 4). First, does it fulfil the need by delivering the water easily and painlessly? Second, are the materials adequate: are they rigid enough, are they impermeable? Third, was the

The Crow and the Bottle

Once upon a time, there was a very thirsty crow. She flew around looking for a river, or a pond, or even a tiny pool of water so she could have a drink. She flew for miles but it was dry and dusty everywhere.

Suddenly, she saw a big bottle shining in a garden. When she landed close by she could see that there was water in the bottle. 'At last!' she thought. 'I'll drink enough for a week!'

The crow pushed her beak as far as it would go into the bottle but she could not reach the water. As everyone knows, crows' beaks are big and fat and bottle necks are small and narrow so, no matter how hard she pushed, she could not have a drink. She tried pulling and tugging at the bottle but the water made it heavy and it would not fall over. The crow was very thirsty now and this might be the only water for miles. She just had to have a drink! What could she do?

(At this point, the children can invent ways of solving the problem and try out their ideas on a plastic bottle half full of water. Afterwards, they can see how the crow solved the problem.)

The crow glanced around the garden. What was there that might help – flowers, grass, soil? None of these seemed useful. Then she noticed a pile of small pebbles. She walked around them, staring and thinking. Suddenly, she picked one up and dropped it into the bottle. The water rose a little. Quickly she dropped in another, and another. Each time, the water rose a little higher until, with one last plop of a pebble, it reached the top of the bottle. The crow sipped the water, drank her fill and flew away.

(Adapted from Aesop's 'The Crow and the Pitcher')

Clever, traditional stories come from all parts of the world. Consider Sanjeev's problem as told in the following adaptation of a traditional Indian tale (see also 'The Brahmin, the Tiger and the Fox' by Surya Kumari in *That'd be Telling*, Michael Rosen and Joan Griffiths, Cambridge University Press, 1985).

themselves to our purpose, it hardly seems worth prising the tiny pearls from those that are reluctant to give them freely. There are also more recent poems and rhymes which can be useful sources in just the same way. For example, in a topic on air, 'Who has seen the wind?' by Christina Rossetti (included in *The Merry-go-Round* by James Reeves, Puffin Books) might be used to set the scene for designing and making a wind detector.

Stories

As with nursery rhymes, there are many traditional short stories read to or by children. Aesop's fables are among the oldest (Aesop was a Greek slave of about 550 BC) and some present interesting problems. Consider the plight of the crow:

Sanjeev, the Tiger and the Fox

Once upon a time, in India, a man called Sanjeev was walking through a forest. As he walked in the shadow of the trees, he came to a clearing where the sun beat down. To his surprise, there was a tiger in the middle of the clearing, sitting in the bright sun. But Sanjeev was quite safe because the tiger was trapped in a cage.

Sanjeev stared at the tiger for a moment then began to walk away because he had important things to do, but the tiger pleaded with him to let him out of the cage. Sanjeev felt so sorry for the tiger that he forgot that tigers can be dangerous. He quickly lifted one end of the cage so that the tiger could escape.

The tiger squeezed through the gap and was free. But now, his pleading mews became fierce, hungry roars as he looked at Sanjeev. Sanjeev's legs were weak with fear but he made them run and climb a tree. The tiger strolled over to the tree, licked his lips, sat on the warm dusty ground and waited.

A short time later, a fox came by.

'Why are you sitting there?' asked the fox.

'I want to eat that man,' growled the tiger.

'I'm the one who freed him from that cage!' Sanjeev complained. 'See how he treats me!'

'I can't believe you would be so silly!' said the fox, staring lazily at Sanjeev in the tree.

'But he was!' said the tiger, with a smile so broad that his sharp teeth gleamed in the sunlight.

'No, it can't be true,' said the fox. 'I have never heard such a silly thing in all my life!'

'Yes it is true!' said the tiger, becoming a little annoyed.

'No, it can't be', replied the fox, mildly. 'People are not so silly.'

'I tell you he did!' the tiger growled, so annoyed that his fur began to stand on end.

'Hmmm!' said the fox, doubtfully.

'Yes, he did!' shouted the tiger, so angry that his tail flicked to and fro and made little clouds of dust spin in the air behind it. 'Look, I'll show you!' he said, furiously, and the tiger crawled into the cage and let it fall behind him. 'Now show this silly fox how you let me out!' he commanded Sanjeev.

The fox gave Sanjeev a big smile as Sanjeev climbed from the tree.

'No!' said Sanjeev firmly. 'You can stay where you are, you ungrateful animal!'

Sanjeev thanked the fox and they both went on their way. The tiger stared after them with smooth fur and drooping tail. He mewed sorrowfully until they were out of sight and then lay down in the hot sun again and waited.

(Explain to the children that it is very cruel to leave an animal in a trap. They should imagine what it must be like with no food and water, sitting in the hot sun and never knowing if they will be free to go home. Suppose they are the next one to walk through that forest and they find the tiger in the cage. How could they help him to escape? They should remember what happened to Sanjeev! Can they invent a safe way to free the tiger, and try it with a model of the cage?)

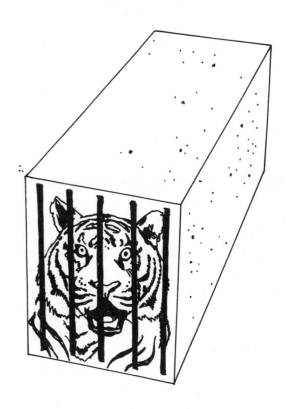

Figure 10.1 Visual stimulus to accompany 'Sanjeev, the Tiger and the Fox', made from a cardboard box

Modern stories can be just as fruitful. For instance, *Katie Morag Delivers the Mail* by Mairi Hedderwick (Picture Lions) is a tale about a little girl in the Highlands who has to help with the mail but meets with a number of difficulties on the way. The children could be invited to invent and make something to help Katie carry the letters across the fast, deep stream between her and their destination. *Burglar Bill* by Janet and Allan Ahlberg (Mandarin Little Mammoth) is a story about a somewhat inept thief who succeeds in stealing a baby in mistake for loot. The children could be asked to invent and make something which would stop Bill from making off with his ill-gotten gains. Similarly, *Adventure Playground* by Helen Burgess (Hodder and Stoughton) might be used to stimulate the children to design and make a model playground to suit their own and their friends' interests. Another possibility which might be used is for children to present a particularly exciting scene in a story in a model theatre. This model theatre could, for example, have a number of moving parts: a working curtain, a sun which rises and sets on the back 'cloth', and articulated players.

Pictures, poems and stories may also be presented through the medium of television. They can be used in the same way as those which are presented to the class in other ways.

Topics and themes

Project work, topics, themes, centres of interest and integrated studies are terms often used to describe essentially the same classroom activity. A range of experiences in different areas of the curriculum and subsumed under a collective heading is offered to the children. The common thread through these experiences is intended to provide unity and relevance to the children's learning. In this way, topics or themes like 'ourselves' and 'caring' might be used to provide activities across the curriculum and this can include technology.

Where teaching is through a topic or theme, the proportion of time allocated to it depends on the school and the teacher. For those who wish to include technology in this approach, some examples of planning webs for popular themes are shown on page 145. Each includes examples of technological activities which might sit comfortably among the others in the theme. Not all themes lend themselves well to cross-curricular work. Some would have to be stretched beyond credibility to give activities for everything. This defeats the search for coherence, unity and relevance. If such limited themes must be used, then those subjects not touched on adequately will have to be provided for in other ways. The technological activities listed could be presented as open or closed problems according to the needs of the pupils. Pupils should, however, have experience of working on open activities.

Key Stage 1

Technology from:	Some activities (and possible outcomes)
Birthdays	• Design and make a birthday card with a pop-up or moving part (**A**) and a message printed using a computer (**IT**). • Make some decorations for a party (**A**). • Plan the menu for a birthday picnic (**E**), including the order in which shops will be visited (**S**) and food prepared (**S**). • Print the menu using a computer (**IT**).
Homes	• Design and make a model house with a door which will open and close (**A**). • Design and make a home corner for the classroom (**E**). • Make an action plan for tidying your bedroom (**S**). • Carry out a survey of the different types of house lived in by children in the class and store the data (**IT**).
My school	• Make a bookmark for your reading book (**A**). • Suggest ideas for storing pencils or crayons (**A**). • Design and make a desk tidy (**A**). • Plan and carry out a survey of visitors to the school. Use it to plan a visitors' waiting area and decide where to put a new 'welcome', mat (**IT and E**).
Ourselves	• Invent something which can be used to scratch your back (**A**). • Make a draw-string bag for PE clothes (**A**). • Make name badges using a word processor (**IT**), • Plan and carry out a survey of children in the class to find their favourite stories. Use a word processing package to write a new story (**IT**).
Road safety	• Invent something which will make you more easily seen when crossing the road (**A**). • Design and make a stop/go signal with a moving part (**A**). • Carry out a survey to decide the best place for a zebra crossing (**IT**). • Write some road safety rules and use IT to print copies for other children in the class (**IT**).
The farm	• Invent something which will help lift sacks of corn (**A or S**). • Design and make a model well with a winding mechanism for lifting the bucket (**S**). • Make a feed tray for the hens (**A**). • Use a concept or overlay keyboard to write an illustrated story about a visit to the farm (**IT**).
Toys	• Design and make a finger or glove puppet (**A**). • Design and make a puppet with a moving part (**S**). • Invent something which can be used to store small toys tidily (**A**). • Plan and carry out a survey of favourite toys in your class (**IT**) and design and make a new one (**A**).
Wheels	• Make a wind-powered land yacht (**A**). • Design and make a free-wheel buggy (**A**). • Invent a way of moving a very large, heavy box from the classroom to the hall (**A or S**). • Invent and make something with wheels to move garden rubbish (**A or S**).

Key: (A) Artefact **(S)** System **(E)** Environment **(IT)** Information Technology

Visits

Most of the time, the children will be in or around the classroom but the world outside offers direct experience, interest, excitement and purpose. 'In the classroom, the most helpful aid is the window, and the most helpful piece of equipment is the door' (D. Waters quoting K. Hoy, Warden of the Waltham Forest Centre, in *Primary School Projects*, Heinemann, 1987). For technology, the outside world illustrates real needs in relevant contexts and real, often tangible solutions for examination and evaluation. However, desultory rambles along by-ways and highways waste the opportunities they present. The teacher must be clear beforehand why the class are going, what they will see and what they will do. As far as the last aim is concerned, this includes preparatory activities before the visit and continuation activities afterwards. Visits with potential for developing technological capability include:

• farms, agricultural and horticultural centres;
• harbours and ports;
• airports, stations;
• supermarkets, shopping centres;
• parks, adventure playgrounds, leisure centres.

By their nature, such visits will require attention to safety and close supervision of the children.

The photo shows a child's handwriting on a board: "Castles used to get their water from wells. We made ... model wells us... pulle... wheels."

Chapter eleven

A progression for Key Stage 2 technology

Design and technology

The example of a progression for Key Stage 2 design and technology which follows was constructed using the rationale described in Chapter Eight and takes into account the requirements of the National Curriculum. There will be some spread of capabilities in any one class and it is very unlikely that all will have reached the same level by the end of Key Stage 1. The progression offered here is intended to fit end-on with that

described for Key Stage 1 in Chapter Nine and continues from it. In gauging what will be appropriate for a given pupil or group of pupils, the teacher will need to take this into account.

Artefacts, systems and environments gives a sequence of technological products to illustrate those that suit this stage. These are only examples of activities and it is not necessary to attempt all or any of those listed, if similar ones, better suited to a topic or resources are available. Within each major division of product (artefact, system and environment) the progression begins with the least demanding tasks. For example, each subsection might be revisited for more complex activities, each term or year, or particular subsections might be dealt with more completely than others in a given term or year, or later subsections might be deferred until a higher level of skill and experience has been accumulated. The subtitles indicate some of the demands made. However, the situation or brief can be used to tune the demand of an activity and different outcomes can be expected from children of different capabilities. For example, supporting a flagpole or a tent could be activities which make much the same demands, but the second could be made more demanding by stipulating that the ground is too stony to allow tent pegs or poles to be hammered in or by demanding a higher level of planning. For that reason, progressions for such aspects as planning are also provided. Pupils should continue to be encouraged to identify needs and, when feasible, design and make a product which satisfies that need. **Working with ideas** gives guidance on progression in that area.

Working with materials describes a progressive sequence of working skills: using tools, joining and finishing. A sequence is also described for working safely and choosing materials.

Satisfying needs and addressing opportunities is about the mental processes of invention: identifying needs, designing to satisfy a need, planning to realise a design, and evaluating outcomes. A progressive sequence is offered for each.

For each of these, the knowledge and understanding a pupil may bring to the activities or develop through them is described. Some experiences which might precede designing and making are suggested. **Working with ideas** describes stages and strategies in generating, developing and communicating ideas.

While these divisions reflect those of the National Curriculum programme of study, some readjustment was found useful in presenting the progression. **Artefacts, systems and environments** confines itself largely to the products of technology, **Working with materials** relates to the practical skills and **Satisfying needs and addressing opportunities** to mental processes. The last division, **Working with ideas**, has been widened to include some discussion on helping pupils generate ideas.

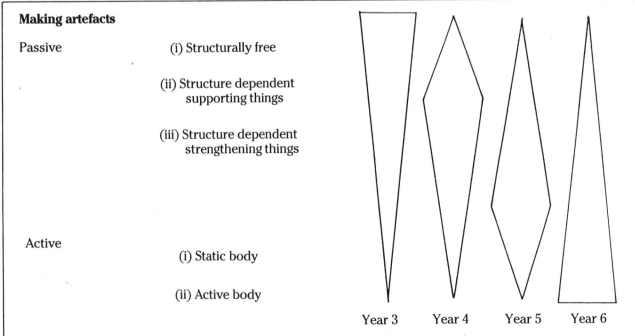

Figure 11.1   No kind of artefact, system or environment is the sole preserve of any one year group but the core of the experience moves through the levels.

148

Using the progression

The examples of artefacts, systems and environments form a progression. With artefacts, for example, younger children could begin with activities like those that head the list and older ones could confine their attentions to those towards the end of the list. As at Key Stage 1, this would be unnecessarily restrictive; there will be active artefacts which younger children might make and passive artefacts appropriate to the capabilities of older pupils. Hard and fast horizontal divisions can be avoided if we think of progression as the movement of the core of experiences through the list, thereby allowing products on either side of the core to be attempted as illustrated in Figure 11.1. The same argument applies to the other systems and environments and to the other progressions.

To illustrate, consider the topic 'transport'. In Year 3, an aspect of this might be water transport and the children might make a pontoon bridge and a lighthouse. Both would require the use of specialist tools, various kinds of joints, a careful choice of materials and finishes which would be waterproof. More information might be needed to allow the designing of a pontoon bridge and procedures might have to be adapted when unexpected difficulties arose.

In Year 4, an aspect of this topic might be road transport and the children could build a suspension road bridge, a wheeled vehicle to run across it and a stop-go sign for each end of the bridge. They might have to make a detailed list of the resources needed and cost them, adjusting their design to suit the fixed amount of money they have been allowed. As a group, pairs of pupils might work on different aspects of the project.

In Year 5, where an aspect might be rail transport, a wooden trestle-work bridge and train to suit might be made. For the bridge, a lever-action signal could also be provided. This would require the use of a variety of specialist tools and, in making the

framework, might call for the adaptation of procedures as difficulties in fabrication are met.

The same topic in Year 6 could lead to a working model of a lifting or swing bridge, a self-propelled vehicle and a computer controlled warning light or signal for the bridge. When brainstorming for ideas on how to make the bridge, several ideas might be fused to produce the design, help might be sought in programming the signal, and the pupils might describe how they will work differently in the future to design and make more effectively.

Procedure

One procedure for devising and selecting an activity could be as follows:
• Choose the kind of artefact, system or

environment which suits the theme or topic in hand and which makes appropriate demands in terms of knowledge, understanding, materials and making skills. Be prepared to use or adapt a pupil's idea, especially where it arises from a need perceived by the pupil.

• Devise a situation, scenario or brief which fits in naturally with the current work and is likely to motivate the pupils. When possible and appropriate, make it open-ended (couching it in such terms as, 'Invent something which will . . .').

• Using the appropriate parts of the progressions for **Working with materials** (using tools, joining, finishing, working safely, using materials), **Satisfying needs and addressing opportunities** (identifying needs, designing to satisfy a need, planning to realise a design, evaluating outcomes) and **Working with ideas** (generating ideas, developing ideas, communicating ideas), clarify what is expected in these areas and, when appropriate, add conditions or constraints or devise a procedure which obliges the pupils to develop and extend their experience.

For example, in Year 3, in a topic on 'pollution', following an attempt to clear the school yard of litter, the Pollution Patrol decide they need a device to pick up litter. This could be passive or active, according to the experience and expectations of the children and the constraints imposed by the teacher.

In Year 4, in a topic on 'birds', the children begin a survey to determine what birds will eat, but find that the playground is not a suitable place to leave the test food. They need to make a bird table in view of the classroom window, but the ground is quite solid there. A pole and board is provided, but they need to strut, stay or buttress their artefact in some way. Careful thought needs to be given to the finish so that the birds are neither injured nor frightened by it.

During Year 5, in a topic on 'weather', it is winter and there is snow outside. The caretaker is having a hard time clearing the snow. What could we make to help him? The answer might be a snow pusher. Other needs which might arise from this topic are for instruments for a weather station (such as a wind direction and a wind speed indicator) so that a scientific record of the weather can be kept each day.

A topic on 'energy' in Year 6 allows pupils to compare ancient and modern ways of doing things. Here they might make a working model of a windmill or water-wheel using an electric motor for a display for a parents' evening. This would be displayed with a tape-recorded account of the project and carefully made labels attached to it by coloured threads, the whole being supervised and demonstrated by its makers.

Key Stage 2

Artefacts, systems and environments

'In each key stage pupils should design and make . . . artefacts . . . systems . . . and . . . environments . . . in response to needs and opportunities identified by them' *(Technology in the National Curriculum, page 19).*

The experiences offered to younger children are extended as their increasing knowledge and skills are put to use. Examples of artefacts, systems and environments are listed separately but this is not to imply that they do not overlap.

In working materials, more ways of joining are made available, and more constraints and factors have to be considered. Structures include three-dimensional rectilinear and other frameworks and inherently strong shapes and structures. Artefacts with moving parts and mechanisms are powered in various ways and some experience of automatic control is offered. The construction of

systems and environments is widened, with more aspects to consider.

The occurrence of an example of a construction technique in one area does not preclude its application in another. For example, the frameworks found in structurally-dependent static artefacts could be used in some active artefacts. It is also possible to devise a teaching sequence which provides experience of frameworks in making, say, a self-propelled buggy. Here, the sequence concentrates largely on one experience at a time and the teacher must judge when and which experiences might be combined.

Note that, for brevity, examples of actual products are listed. This is not to suggest that they should be presented in this form. Situations and contexts may be devised which are likely to lead to products like those. Compare, for instance, 'Make a snow pusher' with 'Invent something to help the caretaker clear the snow'. Each might serve the same function but they offer different experiences.

Making artefacts

Passive

• *Structurally free:* book cover, coloured ink, snow pusher, device to pick up litter, plant waterer, pontoon bridge, refreshments for a fête/party/parents' evening in summer/winter, packed lunch for a class trip, toasted sandwiches for a governors' meeting, winter mittens for a toddler, something to prevent a toddler losing gloves, a stuffed toy for a school fund-raising event, a block printed cushion as a Mother's Day gift, a food cover, an oven glove.

• *Structure dependent; supporting things (such as struts, stays, guys, piers, buttresses):* flag pole, tent, suspension bridge, cantilever bridge.

• *Structure dependent; strengthening things (such as plated joints, arches, domes, corrugations, triangular frameworks):* framework bridges, arched bridges, electricity pylons for a model village (class activity), roof for a model house, protective package for an egg or biscuit.

Active

• *Static body, active parts:* working lighthouse, crank-operated model windmill, model conveyor, crab with grabbing claws, gravity-operated lift, elastic band powered windmill without/with a lever action brake, electric motor powered tower crane, electric motor powered winch which pulls a toy car to it and automatically switches off, computer controlled level crossing.

• *Active body:* train set with shock absorbing bumpers, self-propelled vehicle, electrically-powered vehicle which switches off when it touches a wall, which reverses when it touches a wall, computer controlled vehicle.

Making systems

• *Single process:* as exemplified in active artefacts above (for example the crab and lighthouse).

• *Several processes:* adventure playground, fairground (group activities), school shop, model railways system (class activity).

• *Linear routines:* a plan of action for cleaning a room, a circus of new physical education activities in the hall, nature trail guide, a recipe.

• *Branching routines:* a board game with routes determined by the throw of a dice or coin (for example, if 6 then go to square 22; if heads then go to jail for one go), producing a school newspaper.

Environments

• *Several factors:* a waiting room for visitors to the school, a mother-and-toddlers room in the school, a model of a pleasant, three-storey car park to replace a dark, depressing one which is often full of car fumes, a model of a doctor's waiting room, a model of a leisure centre, a school garden, a garden for blind people.

• *Conflicting factors:* a recreation area for both young and old.

Some experiences which might precede designing and making tasks

• Examine the different ways of strengthening and supporting structures indoors and outdoors (for example, reinforcement with wooden and metal triangles, buttressing of buildings, stays

around telegraph poles, struts under door canopies and shelves, triangular frameworks in bicycles and pylons, the geodesic dome). Make bricks from mud and straw and without straw, visit a brickworks, make miniature bricks from clay and see the results of firing them.

• Compare a range of bridges (directly or in pictures) and find out about the structures used.

• Locate examples of the use of arches, domes and curved surfaces in load-bearing structures (look at a crash helmet, the skull, eggs, corrugated card and steel, and in buildings such as castles, churches, mosques, ice-houses).

• Explore the mechanisms which enable the action of powered toys, observing in particular, the action of such things as gears and belt drives on the speed of rotation of wheels, and how mechanisms transform one form of motion into another. Find out how the energy is stored and controlled. Visit a water-mill and windmill.

• Trace the action of mechanisms in simple, amusing Heath Robinson pictures and draw

their own.

• Construct a schematic map of the organisational structure of the school, the feudal system in the Middle Ages, the class computer system, a hi-fi system, departments in a supermarket. Find out about the digestive system, a filing system, a kitchen system from brochures.

• List the system for playing a board game (for instance, Throw dice; *go to* the square shown by the dice; *if* it is a snake's tail, *then* go to its head; *if* it is a ladder, *then* climb it; *if* neither, *then* stay where you are until your next go).

• Identify the input action, the process and the output action of mechanical and electrical systems they use.

• Explore environments for diverse groups of people and see how needs are met (visit a public library, leisure centre and shopping mall).

• Explore environments where needs are in conflict and some compromise is necessary (smoking and no-smoking provision on public transport, traffic and pedestrian control in the high street).

Some knowledge and understanding of concepts used in the tasks

Force

The effect of the size and direction of a force on the movement of an object and fast moving objects needing more time to stop or a bigger force to stop them than slow moving objects of the same mass. The force of gravity as the pull of the Earth on an object. Weight as a force. The Newton as a unit of force. How to measure force. Friction and forces in balance (for example, a buggy which fails to run down an incline because the force of friction opposing the motion is equal to the force of gravity pulling down the slope). The upthrust on an object in water and factors which determine whether an object floats or sinks.

Energy

The need for a source of energy for a working machine. Fuels as energy sources. The limited nature of energy resources like fossil fuels.

Electricity

Conductors and insulators. The heating and magnetic effects of an electric current. Simple circuit drawings and diagrams. The dangers of mains electricity.

Shape and structure

The strength of triangular frameworks, domes and arches. Stability arising from a wide base and the weight being concentrated near the base.

Control

Mechanical: mechanisms and energy transfer devices involving wheels, levers, linkages, gears, cams, pulleys, belts, pistons (see also **Working with materials**, page 155).

The control of the flow of electricity (how to make a motor go faster or slower). Circuits for measuring, switching and control (for example, the AND and NOT gates).

Materials

See **Working with materials** (page 155).

Working with materials

'Pupils should be taught to take reasonable care at all times for the safety of themselves and of others . . . At each key stage pupils should be given opportunities to work with a range of materials, including textiles, graphic media (such as paint, paper, photographs), construction materials (such as clay, wood, plastic, metal), and food' (*Technology in the National Curriculum*, page 19).

Using tools

Co-ordination, control, accuracy and skill in using tools is developed through regular use; the range of tools is increased (rasp and file, screwdriver, use of an oven with appropriate supervision); tools suited to a particular task are chosen from the range available; consideration is given to the cost of materials and to minimising waste.

Joining

Shaping materials to make joints at angles, for triangular frameworks for instance; making temporary joints with nuts and bolts, permanent joints with screws, temporary joining to allow adjustment (for example, tacking fabrics).

Finishing

Increasing care by tidying threads on a knitted or stitched garment; considering decoration and function of the finish (covering a surface with a soft and attractive material to protect the hands from sharp edges, using a material with rough texture to provide grip, choosing a bright, warning colour so that an artefact is easily seen).

Working safely

Using tools safely and correctly; using safety equipment without prompting; taking some responsibility for safe working (agreeing to and following safety procedures); showing responsibility for own and others' safety, checking the condition of equipment before use, taking action to report or warn if a dangerous situation is perceived.

Choosing materials

Selecting materials for the task in hand based on several factors (cost, availability, purpose, weight and working properties); adjusting the materials to suit the task (strengthening by folding, bending, increasing number to make a carrier bag handle; thickening by increasing the concentration of dyes and paints to produce a monochrome finish in various shades) and avoiding waste (for instance, not cutting a small circle from the centre of a large sheet of card and compacting the pieces to be taken from a length of fabric).

Some experiences which might precede designing and making tasks

• See a variety of tools being used expertly (a visit to a building site, a visit to a brickworks). Guess the purpose of unfamiliar tools (nail punch, device for turning jar lids, seam ripper, tree pruner, screwdriver with a right angled bend or one for holding in a brace and bit). Examine an old agricultural tool in a museum; find out what it was used for and how its job is done today; compare a garden fork for digging with one used for lifting potatoes.

• Examine a range of angled joints (picture frame corners, brick wall corners, braced and bracketed fixings such as shelves, dovetailed joints in drawers). Dismantle and assemble an artefact with nut and bolt or screw joints; dismantle an artefact with nailed joints; compare the two.

• Look for pattern in nature (snowflakes, honeycombs) and use them in decorative finishes such as wallpaper designing. Identify matt and gloss finishes in the classroom and compare their visual and physical properties, relating them to their use. Examine a range of objects designed to be gripped firmly and which exemplify a range of textural finishes (pen shank, knurled knob of a clock, door handle). See objects where texture is decorative and used for visual contrast, for instance, in metal artefacts such as tea pot, lamp and watch strap. Compare the textures of natural materials (wood, stone, marble, brick and so on).

• Compile a list of safety rules for technology and list them so that their initial letters form an appropriate word (for example, *safety* and *technology*). Examine a range of materials which have been adjusted to alter their properties (plywood, fibreboard, plasterboard, toffee and fudge, garments made from bias cut material). Examine a commercially produced pattern for making a garment or a cast or stamped sheet of parts for a toy or model to see how waste is minimised and cost reduced by using material economically.

Some knowledge and understanding of concepts used in the tasks

• Properties of materials determined by tests related to their uses (strength, hardness, flexibility, solubility, rigidity). Softness of dough; consistency of mix. The working properties of materials (paper and card, plastics, hardwood, softwood, aluminium sheet, clay, flour and water mixes, fabrics). Effect of sunlight and micro-organisms on materials.

• Solids, liquids and gases as having mass and volume. Compressibility of gases exemplified by air.

• Changes of state resulting from heating and cooling (melting, boiling, freezing, condensing).

• Solutions, separating and purifying mixtures.

• Acids and alkalis.

• Permanent changes brought about by processing materials as seen in making plaster of Paris, concrete and firing clay.

• Natural materials and their uses (sands, soils, rocks and minerals).

• Dangerous materials such as bleach and hot oil.

• The purpose of particular tools and the way they work.

Satisfying needs and addressing opportunities

'As pupils progress, they should be given more opportunities to identify their own tasks for activity and should use their knowledge and skills to make products which are more complex, or satisfy more demanding needs' (*Technology in the National Curriculum*, page 19).

Identifying needs

Operate with more independence when recognising needs in familiar situations (for instance, turning a complaint or grumble into a statement about a need). When evaluating an existing product, see an opportunity for improvement and propose simple, practical modifications. Identify needs and opportunities in progressively less familiar situations, initially with guidance on strategies when necessary and later with more independence and more systematic searches (the need for a bus shelter, being advised to find where they are normally placed and the factors which need to be considered, for example). Use a wider range of sources of information, such as carrying out a survey to find out where people feel a litter bin or a bus shelter should be situated, or using a questionnaire to identify classmates' preferences concerning a new playground. Identify those needs which are not feasible for various reasons (playground equipment which is too big or too costly). Be able to justify their conclusions when identifying needs.

Designing to satisfy a need

Take account of needs and values arising from the variety of backgrounds and cultures that there are. Review a design to identify what still needs to be decided or solved (how the battery is to be held in place on a self-propelled buggy, whether it would be better to use buttons or a zip fastener on a pyjama case). Collect more information to allow designing to proceed. List the resources needed, including the approximate amounts and check that they are available, altering the design to suit availability, when necessary. Fuse together parts of two or more designs to produce a more effective one. Consider any unwelcome consequences if the proposed product is made.

Planning to realise a design

Prepare a sequential plan or flow diagram for the making activity. If working in a group, decide who will make what parts of the product. Prepare a branching plan when a part of the product cannot be worked for a while (consider making another part of the product while the paint dries on the first part). Adapt procedures when difficulties arise. Seek help when difficulties become insurmountable.

Evaluating outcomes

Evaluate the product against the design brief or the need and suggest improvements (testing that an oven glove fits, is heat resistant and looks good, suggesting that it might be better with a tongue extending up the inside of the arm). Consider how others might view the product and how cost-effective it is. Describe in what ways their designing and making might be performed better in the future. Evaluate at each stage of the making process and adapt and adjust before proceeding.

Some experiences which might precede designing and making tasks

• Compare and contrast different versions of a product from the point of view of their aesthetic qualities (birthday cards, scarves). Compare traditional patterns on fabrics such as rugs and survey people's preferences. Rank soaps according to preferred colour and smell, and to weight and effectiveness and compare the results with the prices. Test a range of paint brushes similarly. Visit a Victorian or Georgian house and compare it with a modern house.

• Identify markets for goods and services (through a 'Who is it that needs a . . .' game).

• Measure the heights of a number of different doors, tables (floor to surface), chairs (floor to seat), and find their averages; account for the results. Feel the size and weight of a brick and account for them.

• Discuss the effect of design and technology activity on the environment (motorway construction on farmland, flooding of valleys for a dam, landscaping a derelict site). Look at problems from the other person's point of view (for example, what must it be like to live near an airport, or a fishmeal factory?).

• Find out how design and technology have altered life styles (compare eating habits and meals of the nineteenth century with those of today; write a story about what it would be like without electricity, compare the coal fire and kitchen range of the first half of this century with the central heating of a modern home).

• Examine simple plans of new houses in the neighbourhood.

• Use the assembly instructions provided with a product to make it (a kit for a model aeroplane, a cut-out-and-assemble activity from the back of a cereal box). Evaluate the instructions and improve them.

• In a group, evaluate a range of products, such as different makes of coloured pencil, and compile a 'Which' report on them.

• Find out about the life and work of great inventors (Isambard Kingdom Brunel [bridges, ships, railways], George and Robert Stephenson [bridges, ships, mining, railways], Margaret Knight [inventor of the satchel-bottomed paper bag for shops], Verena Holmes [safety guillotine]).

158

Some knowledge and understanding of concepts used in the tasks

• Know that designing and the production of goods and services are influenced by the needs and preferences of the user.

• Know that people are not obliged to use a particular product and that quality, cost and appearance influence their decision.

• Know that ergonomics – taking into account the size, shape, comfort and movement of people in design – is important in designing for people. Similar factors must be considered when designing for other living things.

• Know that costs involve more than the price of materials in the product (the cost of the waste, time, people's skills, equipment).

• Know that mass production reduces costs while custom-made, one-off items and prototypes tend to be relatively expensive to produce.

• Know what advertising is and what its aims are.

• Know that the same problem might be solved in different ways in different cultures and in other periods of time.

• Know what is meant by stock control and stock rotation.

Working with ideas

Generating ideas

The strategies introduced to younger children should be practised and supplemented by others. These would also be deployed in increasingly unfamiliar situations. By definition, such situations imply a degree of ignorance of the context which must be made good. At first, the teacher might point to significant areas of knowledge, understanding and skills which might need to be developed. Later, some responsibility must devolve to the pupil.

First, there is the problem of finding needs and identifying opportunities for technological activity. Often, the teacher will have set a scene which makes a need or

opportunity more or less apparent and will have a particular, educational aim. Another strategy is for children to collect their own and other people's complaints about products in a complaints box or notebook. An alternative is to keep a complaints diary in which they record 'What went wrong with things today' and 'Something that was really needed today'. Older children can sometimes identify needs and opportunities from stories of misadventure and misfortune in a local newspaper. Unlike the teacher's carefully tailored scenario, some of the problems these strategies produce may be beyond the resources of the classroom and the capabilities of the children but their relevance is often unquestionable.

When an appropriate problem or opportunity has been selected, the next task is to clarify it. One way is to ask questions. Here, the teacher's role will depend on the experience and abilities of the pupil. Sometimes it may be necessary to prompt and hint at the relevant question (Do you think it might help if we knew . . .?). At other times, it might be more appropriate to direct the children to appropriate sources of information: books, surveys, interviews and questionnaires. In either case, it helps to make the situation concrete with, for example, the pan with the broken handle on display, a visit to the corner of the school field where the nature reserve is to be, a photograph of an oven for which an oven glove is to be made. Describing and explaining the problem to others often helps to clarify or highlight areas of uncertainty.

Developing ideas

Taking the measure of a problem often leads to germs of ideas for its solution. These may be developed and supplemented by such strategies as brainstorming and, where appropriate, role play. Older children might keep a track of possible solutions with a simple ideas map. Here the problem is stated very simply and briefly in the centre of a sheet of paper in a circle (in words or with a picture) and the ideas are noted around it as they occur, each in a circle. Similar ideas are joined by lines to make different kinds of solutions apparent. Some, after a little thought, may be fused into another solution with more potential than the first generation. Lines would lead from the parent ideas to the new circle. This way of working helps to focus minds and records a store of ideas for later reference should insurmountable difficulties arise.

Likely solutions to the problem may now be considered in the light of resources, skills and knowledge needed, and cost. A promising solution may be selected and sketched in more detail. Where there are no 'special bits' involved (that is, areas of uncertainty), it may be possible to complete the design and proceed straight to the making stage, otherwise these special bits need to be clarified. Pupils should be taught to divide and conquer as a matter of routine. For example, in making a powered fan to produce a cool breeze in summer, the task might be divided into gathering material for the fan blades (light card), deciding how to fix the blades to an axle (using a cork), designing a body for the blades and axle (a framework made from wood), working out how to spin the axle (using an electric motor); solving the *sub-problem* of how to link the spin of the motor to the axle (elastic band) and revising the design by making the framework longer to hold the motor and battery.

Sometimes, it is appropriate to model the solution first. For example, a paper and card model of the nature reserve might be put on view and classmates' opinions and suggestions collected. This could lead to a modified design, such as adding a log to sit

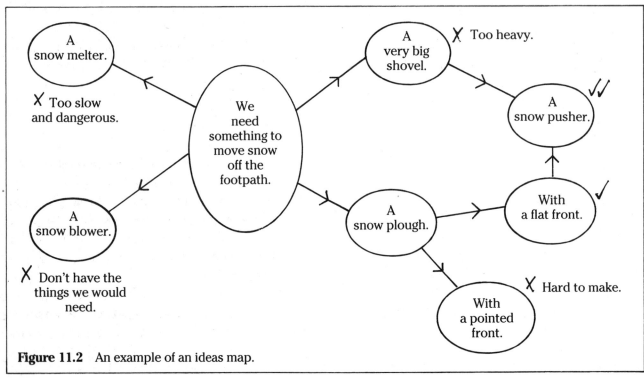

Figure 11.2   An example of an ideas map.

160

on in warm weather. Modelling does not always have to be of the whole product and could be of a crucial part only to check that the idea will work. Kits are often useful for this.

There should also be opportunities for older pupils to see that there are often subsidiary objectives in designing as well as the prime one of making something which does what it should. For example, the fan will gather dust and its blades may be damaged when not in use. How is it to be stored?

Communicating ideas

Older pupils need to build on and practise the ways of communicating already introduced. The production of annotated drawings (monochrome and colour) with written explanations may be by hand or with the help of a computer. Plan views, elevations and sections of simple products need to be introduced to extend the explanatory ability of the representational picture. These may be exemplified by the advertising literature of a local building firm. Flow diagrams showing step by step routines and procedures may accompany a model or artefact, illustrated by the instruction leaflets which accompany many commercially produced artefacts.

Earlier, models were devices to think with and articulate ideas, now they are primarily to communicate an idea to others. For example, a static model might depict a design for a library corner and have coloured threads linking parts of the model to labels. A tape recording beside the model describes the problem and the solution shown, taking each label as a starting point and proceeding clockwise around the display.

Communication is hindered by imprecise denotations like 'thingummy' and 'whatsit'. Vocabulary should keep pace with the development of technological capability so that there is a firm basis for communication. Asking pupils to give a short presentation of their latest project is

a strategy which can be used to practise vocabulary and disseminate new words to the class at large.

Information Technology

The example of a progression for Key Stage 2 information technology which follows was constructed using the rationale outlined in Chapter Eight and takes into account the requirements of the National Curriculum.

For each of the strands of information technology capability, a general indication of demand made by task complexity, situation familiarity, skill level, degree of dependence expected, and level of software sophistication is given. In order to clarify the levels of demand and to illustrate a progression, short sequences of activities are offered. It should be emphasised that these are illustrative, not prescriptive.

Using the progression

Resources vary from school to school and class to class so, while the activities listed will often be feasible, others may be devised and fitted in as appropriate. To this end, the National Curriculum recommends that a chart of available software be compiled, as illustrated earlier (Figure 9.2 on page 132).

Procedure

• For a given topic, list the activities and experiences relating to design and technology and other curriculum areas.
• From the list, identify opportunities to develop particular strands of information technology capability.
• Structure those opportunities so appropriate activities like those in the progression for which software is available are integrated with them.
• Check for or devise opportunities to develop other aspects of information

technology awareness, as described in the **Applications and effects** strand (page 166) and by activities which do not involve direct use of the computer. (When the hardware is in use with one group, it may be possible to pursue alternative aspects with other groups of children.)

For example, on the topic of 'transport', Year 3 children might describe a visit; use an adventure game about a journey; try an electrically-powered boat in an aquarium; and use a switch to operate the light of their lighthouse model. Year 4 could make STOP-GO labels for their road sign; record the results of a traffic survey; and operate a radio-controlled car. Year 5, on the other hand, might prepare an excursion train itinerary; control an electrical train set; and discuss the use of ticket-vending machines and ticket-operated barriers in railway stations. Year 6 could produce a short story about a sea journey for Year 3; prepare a questionnaire on the nuisance of traffic noise and collate the results with the help of a computer; use a programme to model a journey by a vehicle with the aim of minimising fuel consumption; and some

might make computer-controlled traffic lights or control a powered vehicle with the help of a computer.

In places, the National Curriculum programme of study implies that children will set the controls of electrical equipment which operates from the mains supply (tape recorder, microwave oven). The teacher needs to consider if and under what conditions such tasks are appropriate, bearing in mind the safety of the children and the need for them to respect the mains electrical supply.

Developing ideas and communicating information

Information technology is described as a medium for enhancing and extending the experiences of writing, drawing and painting. The keyboard is not intended to replace other ways of producing text, illustration and self-expression. It is to be seen as one means of doing so having, like the other means, its own advantages and limitations.

Task, situation, skill, dependence and software

Pupils should become independent in following their routine procedures, such as loading and using familiar software and in entering information. The passages they produce are expected to be longer, more varied, and any one might include a greater range of information than at Key Stage 1. Type sizes and styles might be changed and a normal keyboard used to produce text. The software might be the same as before but more of its capacity would be used, otherwise more options might be made available to the pupil.

Activities
• Produce a narrative style class news-sheet, listing the events of the day or week in the order in which they occurred.

• Give an account of a visit to a farm, wildlife park, castle, and so on and illustrate it with pictures taken from a databank or by using a simple draw facility.
• Prepare the insert for a greetings card.
• Prepare headed notepaper for writing a letter.
• Design and make seating arrangement labels for a party.
• Produce a class news-sheet with the events in the order in which they occurred, then edit it so that the most significant appears first and is emphasised in some way.
• Prepare descriptive labels for wall displays.
• Design and make certificates for sports days.
• Write a letter to a friend or relative.
• Design and make a bookplate.
• Produce a class news-sheet in which the events are ordered according to importance, provided with headlines, and with a regular place for such news as today's weather.
• Produce an information schoolfax screen for a parents' evening, giving directions and the times of events.
• Produce copies of an information note about the date of a school holiday to be sent to all parents from the headteacher.
• Write an itinerary for a visit.
• Produce a class news-sheet set out like a newspaper, including places for regular features, short letters, announcements such as birthdays and holiday dates.
• Produce an illustrated short story for younger children.
• Edit and print copies of a ticket or leaflet for a PTA event, prepare a brochure for a carol service or school concert.
• Write a letter requesting information.

Handling information

Information handling refers to the computer's ability to store, sort, organise and otherwise process information. The ability to manipulate information is important, but so is asking the right

questions and knowing if they have been answered. By taking some of the burden of manipulation, the computer frees the pupil to practise and develop such capabilities.

Task, situation, skill, dependence and software

Tasks may involve entering several pieces of information per record, using a database and analysing data. Situations will often be familiar but may extend into less familiar but meaningful areas. Independence would be shown with familiar software and would develop fairly readily with new, appropriate packages.

Activities

• Collect information and enter it in a database for later use (data on the kinds and numbers of vehicles passing the school on the hour throughout the day, later identifying when lorries are more common; similarly, data from a survey of minibeasts at the same time on different days to see

when minibeasts are most likely to be found and which are more common in dry weather, and which are more common in damp weather, data from a survey of local habitats like a wood, pond, school field).
• Record personal information (name, hair colour, eye colour, sex, shoe size, and so on) and extract from it subsets by hand (for example, the names of all boys with blue eyes). Subsequently repeat the exercise using a computer with other information of this nature and note advantages and disadvantages of using this method.
• Examine a hard copy of the information in a prepared file of partially incorrect personal information about themselves (name, address, date of birth, hair colour) and correct the information in the file.
• Examine examples of incorrect data entry in everyday life (such as incorrectly addressed labels).
• Construct a questionnaire about likes or dislikes (sweets, pets, indoor games). Survey classmates' likes and dislikes and record the results. Extract subsets (the number of people who like jelly sweets or blue party hats). Consider how this might affect their plans for a party.
• Examine the results of the processing of incorrect information in a database, identify implausible results and locate the source of

the error (either arising from the pupils' own work or using a prepared file of, for example, data on the heights of classmates with one entry being so large that it makes the average height very unlikely, or similarly treating data on the number of bird visitors to the playground each day).
• Design a questionnaire to do with parents' shopping preferences (where, what, why). Try it out on the adults in school and revise the questions to make them more effective. Issue the revised questionnaire to parents and enter the results into a database. Use the database to produce a summary of and conclusions about shopping patterns.
• Compile a database for the classroom library and maintain it.

Modelling

The computer can be used to model or simulate events in the real or in an imaginary world.

Task, situation, skill, dependence and software

Pupils will interact with computer simulations of classroom and other meaningful activities or events linked to a cross-curricular topic or theme or curriculum focus and relate outcomes to the real world. Interaction could be in a variety of ways such as keyboard, menu, mouse or joystick. The software would present a clearly defined objective, tasks might involve several options and there may be the need for a simple manipulation of information and speculation about outcomes and their consequences.

Activities

• Use a simple adventure program and discuss how it responds to the pupil's decisions, looking particularly for predictable responses.
• Use a computer game prior to and as an analogy for a physical phenomenon (for example, the bouncing of a ball in computer tennis and the reflection of light from a mirror).

• Use game-like programs which simulate practical situations and have a clear objective (controlling the temperature in the rooms of a house under changing weather conditions, running a flour-producing mill).
• Use a computer simulation of an activity the pupils are doing in science and compare the outcomes (shadow the growth of a seedling with a computer simulation of the event, alter the volume and weight of an object until it floats).
• Simulations of phenomena beyond common experience (comets, the Solar System, eclipses).
• Use a computer simulation to produce the 'best' result by manipulating variables and test the outcome practically, for instance by looking at the best growing conditions for a seedling.
• Use a simulation to observe interacting factors and note any patterns which occur (predator-prey simulations for example).

Some pupils may use a computer language such as LOGO to produce a sample program.

Measurement and control

Computers do not have to be mere passive receivers of information from a keyboard. With the help of a variety of sensors they can automatically collect information about the real world, record and process it and deliver the results on demand. Neither need the flow of information be only inwards; the computer can send instructions out to devices to make them perform complex operations. Put the two together and the computer may be used to measure, gauge or monitor a situation and respond to it with appropriate instructions.

Task, situation, skill, dependence and software

Pupils would use electronic devices and software to record data and would see that the computer may be used to control events and devices. They would learn to

compile a set of commands to control a robot or image on a screen and some would compile programmes to control models.

Activities

• Program an electronic toy or robot to proceed from point A to point B to point C on an open floor (A, B and C not being on a straight line and the distances AB and BC not being equal). Investigate whether the order of the instructions matters in reaching B and in reaching C.
• Use turtle graphics to draw a picture of rectilinear objects like a house. Alter the order of instructions and see what it produces.
• Identify examples of computer controlled systems such as a burglar alarm system. Find out the role of the components of the system (movement sensor, heat sensor, input wires to processor, output wires to alarm unit, alarm unit).
• Observe the action of a time switch used to operate a table lamp automatically in various patterns (the patterns set by the pupil and the connection to mains made by the teacher).
• Detect and measure environmental changes using sensors attached to a computer (heat and light) and monitor how these change with time.
• Use a computer to control a light incorporated into a model made from a kit

(switch a lighthouse on and off; construct a predetermined pattern for the light; compile repeating routines).

• Use a computer to control an electric motor built into a model made from a kit (switching a motor-driven roundabout on and off; operating the roundabout in a predetermined pattern such as, on for five seconds, off for two seconds; compile repeating patterns, refine the program to produce slow for five seconds, fast for two seconds, off for three seconds).

• Make an electrically-operated artefact without a kit and control it with a computer (for example, a buggy).

Some pupils may use information technology to control more complex models such as traffic lights.

Applications and effects

Applications of information technology are widespread, diverse and of various degrees of sophistication. In some cases, they have replaced earlier ways of doing things; in others, they do more than was feasible before and they do new things. The effects are not always simple or obvious. As far as the quality of life is concerned, there may be gains and losses.

Task, situation, skill, dependence and software

Applications in a wider range of situations would be brought to the pupils' attention.

They would contrast these applications and their own use of information technology, with other ways of doing things, identifying advantages and disadvantages of each. They would learn that information may be fallible however it is stored, processed or displayed.

Activities

• Examine an overlay keyboard used in a shop (one which has keys for vegetables, meat and so on). Discuss how this information would be useful to the shopkeeper.

• Where pupils' records are kept on computer file, it may be possible for a pupil to have access to his or her file and see it being updated in some way. They could be asked to check the spelling of their names, their addresses and dates of birth.

• Make a collection of junk mail, classify it and discuss the aims of the senders. Discuss how they might obtain and store lists of names and addresses. Make a collection of computer processed mailing labels addressed to the school.

• Read about information technology inventors such as Charles Babbage and his calculating engine. Compare calculators throughout time (abacus, counting table, slide rule, mechanical calculators, early and recent electronic calculators).

• Choose a task for which it is necessary to use the computer, complete a 'booking' slip and justify why information technology is more appropriate than other means of doing the task.

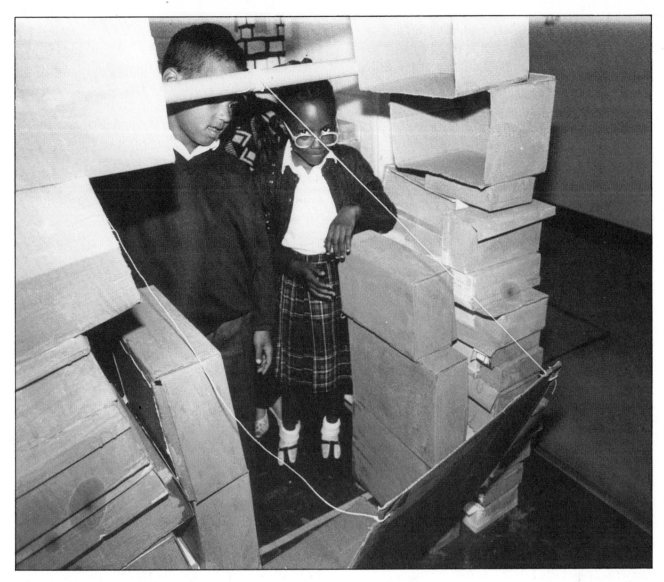

Chapter twelve

Starting points: Key Stage 2

Pictures, poems and stories

Pictures, poems and stories can also be used in Key Stage 2 to set the scene or present a need for technological activity. For instance, a picture from a newspaper which highlights the need for an artefact to help the disabled, material about crime and fire prevention, house plans from estate agents, artist's impressions of proposed developments and pictures of environments such as a bird sanctuary, zoo or wildfowl park may be used to focus thought and stimulate ideas for designing and making activities. Pictures, of course, may also be used to extend a pupil's awareness of particular kinds of technology, like shell and framework structures in buildings.

Some poems lend themselves similarly to presenting a need or opportunity for technological activity. For example, 'The Scarecrow' by Walter de la Mare (*Oxford Book of Poetry for Children*, Oxford University Press, 1963) might be used to stimulate the pupils to design and make a more effective bird scarer which has moving parts. With care, it is even possible to use a nursery rhyme. For instance, we might ask 'Do you remember the Jack and Jill story? A hundred years ago, there were lots of people who had to use wells for water. Suppose it had been you, what would you have done to make life easier for yourself?' Although the starting point is essentially the same as with younger children, the outcome should reflect a higher level of technological capability.

Occasionally, a song might be used to set the scene for a problem to solve. In a topic on 'transport', the pupils might be reminded of the story of the great London Bridge catastrophe:

London Bridge is falling down,
Falling down, falling down.
London Bridge is falling down,
My fair lady.

Here, the solution to a problem exists but, for one reason or another, it is defective; in short, the bridge is about to collapse. What can we do about it? The existing solution could be scrapped and an alternative found. This would be to work through the processes in the sequence: need, design, make and evaluate. However, a useful variation would be to take the faulty bridge as given, then determine and rectify the problem. The problem with the bridge needs to be eliminated. The existing solution has to be evaluated, some remedy must be designed, made and, in turn, evaluated. Evaluation here is not merely a terminal exercise; it is used to determine the nature of the solution.

One way of presenting the problem would be to bridge a gap with card which sags as toy cars are driven over it and the bridge might even be induced to collapse under a particularly heavy car. We might explain that, since London Bridge was built, vehicles have become heavier, now it is expected to support the weight of great pantechnicons. Short of building another bridge, is there anything we might do to reduce the problem?

Working with models, children can often solve problems without regard to scale. Here, the first suggestion might be to place a brick under the span so that it will not sag but the difficulty of obtaining a brick 100m long, not to mention the hazard it presents to river traffic must be brought to their attention. The children are obliged to devise some sort of support, suspension or stiffening system which is in accord with the scale of the model. Threads replace steel hawsers, straws become steel tubes and stiffeners are made from thin card. When the supposed remedy is complete, London Bridge is ready for testing with the same car which induced failure earlier.

In the same way, stories may continue to provide technological activities. For example, *The Wonderful Weathercock* by Roy Brown (Edward Arnold) might be used to point to the need for instruments to monitor the weather, *Mr Lively's Lighthouse* by Antonia Feitz (Angus and Robertson) could lead to the making of a working, model lighthouse and, of course, the *Professor Branestawm Stories* by Norman Hunter (Puffin) might serve to remind the pupils that invention has a humorous side.

Topics and themes

As described in Chapter Ten, a topic approach may be used to give coherence and unity to the experiences provided for the pupils. By Key Stage 2, there is often a gradual transition from general topics to more focused work, especially in the core areas of mathematics, English and science. Investigation, research, manipulation, creation and communication are also developed and refined at this level. All are skills or capabilities fundamental to technological activity. Some examples of planning webs for this key stage can be found on page 169. The technological activities listed could be presented as open or closed problems according to the needs of the pupils. Pupils should, however, have experience of working on open activities.

Key Stage 2

Technology from:	Some activities (and possible outcomes)

Birds
- Design and make a feeding table for birds (**A**).
- Invent something which will keep bird food dry yet release the food to birds as needed (**A**).
- Plan and carry out a survey of bird visitors to the school grounds: use IT to store, amend and retrieve the data (**IT**); use the information to choose where to site a bird table (**A**).

Celebrations
- Design and make a card for a special occasion which has at least one moving part (**A**).
- Suggest ideas for a Mother's Day gift; select one and make it (**A**).
- Plan a party for a special occasion; include invitations (**IT**), decorations, food and entertainment (**A**, **S**, **E**).

Communications
- Invent a way of sending messages from one classroom to another without sending a person (**A** or **S**).
- Invent something to let people know whether or not the headteacher is busy in his or her room (**A** or **S**).
- Use IT to write an illustrated brochure describing the school for new parents (**IT**).

Leisure
- Invent a game for a summer fair (**A** or **S**).
- Design and make a model adventure playground with six different activities (**A**, **S**, **E**).
- Plan and carry out a survey of what local people would like in a new leisure centre (**IT**); design and make a model centre (**E**).
- Use a computer adventure game (**IT**).

Minibeasts
- Invent something which can be used to collect minibeasts without harming them (**A** or **S**).
- Design and make homes for different minibeasts (**A** or **E**).
- Survey minibeasts in different habitats around the school and prepare a report using word processing (**IT**).
- Use IT to make descriptive labels for a minibeast frieze (**IT**).

Shopping centre
- Invent a device for picking up litter (**A**).
- Use IT to design and print anti-litter notices (**IT**).
- Plan and carry out a survey of goods sold in different shops (**IT**); use the information to plan a route to buy goods for a particular purpose (eg Hallowe'en Party) (**S**).
- Design and make a model 'pedestrian-only' shopping centre (**E**).

Travel and transport
- Make a model bridge which can move (**A** or **S**).
- Design and make self-propelled vehicle to carry an object across the school hall (**A** and **S**).
- As a class, design and make a model railway with a station (**S**, **E**).
- Invent something which will carry a container of water across an uneven surface without spilling it (**A** or **S**).

Winter weather
- Design and make something to help prevent a small child from losing her or his winter mittens (**A**).
- Design and make a snow-pusher (**A**).
- Invent something which can be used to store the class's wet wellingtons after playtime without mixing them up (**A** or **S**).

Key: (**A**) Artefact (**S**) System (**E**) Environment (**IT**) Information Technology

Visits

Purposeful visits remain a useful source of technological experience and activity. At this stage, as well as an overall view of a situation, attention will be focused on some complex details, comparisons with the past might be made, and links with other situations indicated. Some examples of visits with technological content are:
• building and construction sites;
• industrial sites and factories;
• industrial heritage museums (eg general, farming, windmills, water-mills);
• historic monuments (eg castles, churches);
• printing works.

Attention to safety, especially in places of work, is essential. Such sites should never be visited without the prior knowledge, permission and advice of those in charge.

Challenges

Challenges may be made to pupils of any age but are particularly motivating for older ones. In essence, technological challenges are usually teacher-initiated and child-resolved. The challenge might be described at the outset and all subsequent work is directly or indirectly aimed at solving it. Alternatively, the challenge might come at the end of a topic or other period of learning and be used to bring skills and knowledge together through their application. The children may work alone, in pairs or larger groups.

Although usually motivating, challenges vary in their apparent relevance. At one end of the spectrum are puzzles and parlour games of doubtful value: 'Who can balance six nails on the head of another nail?' There are the exciting 'egg-race' challenges: 'Who can build the tallest tower from 50 straws to hold a marble at the top?', 'Who can make an egg-carrying buggy which will crash into a wall without breaking the egg?' Such challenges tend to conceal any relevance from the pupil. If this kind of challenge is used, then its relationship to the real world – the structure of a real tower, the protection of a passenger in a car – needs to be indicated. Further along the scale are challenges which include a context such as: 'Build a moonbuggy to carry a supply of water safely over the rough, lunar landscape'. At the other end of the spectrum also, there are the real challenges: 'How can we keep the plants watered over Easter when the school is closed?', 'What are we going to do about the Christmas Party?', 'The caretaker keeps losing his keys and he has asked us to invent something to help him'.

Spontaneous technology

Many of the situations for developing technological capability will be planned and contrived by the teacher. On occasions, some unexpected event may point to a need or opportunity for technology which the children might address. These events might occur in school (the bird table has rotted at the base and fallen over) or out of school (a new park is planned nearby). Opportunities like these should be seriously considered since their relevance to the real world is very apparent. Sometimes such events can be engineered so that they appear to be unexpected. For instance, a teacher might wait for convenient time to complain about the state of the exercise book covers and demand that the children do something about it.

Section three Technological information

This section offers a few, brief notes on selected topics. They are not lessons to be taught to children but are meant to provide information which could help the teacher to develop suitable activities. Some of the topics describe important products of science used in technology, like force, energy and the properties of materials. Others are about these products of technology, like systems, mechanisms and hydraulics, which tend to lie outside common knowledge.

Chapter thirteen

Aspects of technology

Electricity and electronics

A piece of wire consists of billions of *atoms*. Around these atoms are tiny particles called *electrons*. If the wire is merely lying on a table, the electrons in it will be drifting about in a somewhat random way. But when its ends are fastened to a battery, the electrons begin to move through the wire. It is as though the battery has lifted one end of the wire so that the electrons run down its length, then pumped them up to the top for another circuit (Figure 13.1). This flow of electrons is called an *electric current*. If a lot of current flows through the wire, or if the wire is thin, it can become hot. The filament of a light bulb is made thin so that it becomes hot and gives off light. It is difficult for electrons to pass through air so a *break* in the circuit cuts off the current and the bulb goes out. A switch is merely a convenient way of breaking a circuit.

Figure 13.1   The electrical circuit

Switches and gates

In a torch, there is usually a switch. This switch is normally off and the light comes on when it is pressed. Another kind of switch is used on car door frames. When this is pressed (by closing the door), the interior light goes off. In this case, the light is *not* on when the switch is pressed (Figure 13.2)

A door bell might have two switches, one at the front door and another at the back door. When one switch *or* the other is pressed, the bell rings. To turn a light on in a room, again two switches are needed: one at the mains supply and one on the wall. But this time, the arrangement is different so that the light comes on when both the mains switch *and* the wall switch are pressed (Figure 13.3a and b).

Figure 13.2   The circuit for the interior light of a car uses a NOT switch

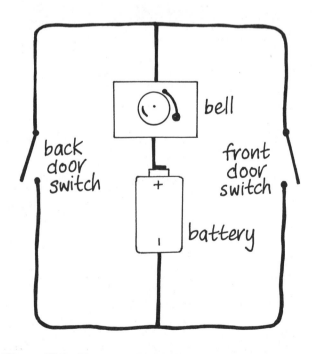

Figure 13.3a   Two switches for a door bell: an OR circuit.

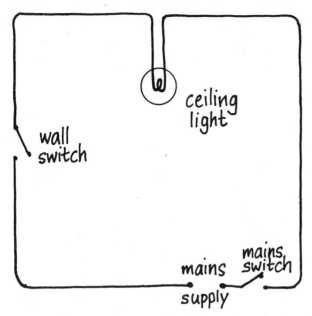

Figure 13.3b House lighting and the mains switch: an AND circuit.

Each of these manual switches has its automatic equivalent in electronics. The automatic versions are called *gates*. There is a NOT gate which is normally open for electricity to flow until it is pressed, then it is not open, hence its name. There is an OR gate which opens when one or the other input is on. There is also an AND gate which opens only when both inputs are on. How this is done is less important here than how to use them. Packaged appropriately, electronic units like these gates can be connected together like building blocks to produce a system which gives the desired result (Figure 13.4). Each block has its own task to do in the system (see also **Systems**, page 189).

A child cannot see electrons flowing through a wire so he or she will benefit from being provided with a concrete analogy. The pump from a soap dispenser serves as a battery and a transparent, viscose tube becomes the wire (Figure 13.5). Water and air bubbles in the tube can be pumped around the circuit and seen as they move. Working the pump vigorously is like having a stronger battery with a bigger voltage; it makes the current increase.

Switches of various kinds are easy to make with foil, drawing pins and thick card.

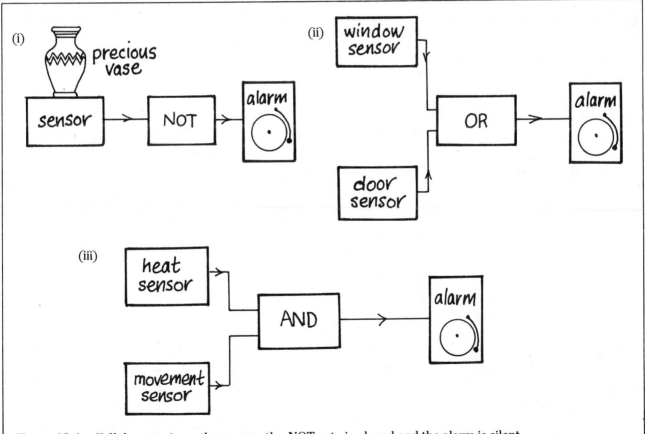

Figure 13.4 (i) If the vase is on the sensor, the NOT gate is closed and the alarm is silent.
(ii) When either the window or the door sensor detects something, the OR gate opens and alarm rings.
(iii) When both heat and movement are detected, the AND gate opens and the alarm rings.

Children should use switches in various ways as needed in their designing and making. Electronic building blocks designed for use in technology are available from several sources.

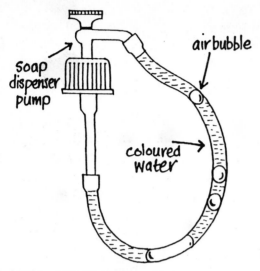

Figure 13.5 A water circuit makes a visible analogy for the electrical circuit: the pump is a little like a battery and the flow of water is like the electrical current.

Energy

To a scientist, energy is *the capacity to do work* but we tend to use the term rather loosely and say such things as 'glucose is full of energy', and 'energy can be stored in a battery'. The impression this fosters is that energy is some sort of invisible material which we can pack into the spaces in glucose and a battery the way we soak a sponge with water. But a sponge without water is still a sponge, while glucose and batteries without their energy are very different. A looser but potentially more meaningful definition for young children is that *energy is something waiting to change and, when it does, we can sometimes make it do something useful for us.*

An elastic band lying limp on the floor, has little that is waiting to change. Prod and poke it and it will simply lie there, inert. Stretch it and that is a different matter. Now there is something waiting to change – if we let it. Point it at the back of a light buggy and release the band. It changes its length and, as it does so, it makes the trolley move a little. We can make it do more (that is, make the process more efficient) by using it like a catapult (Figure 13.6).

In both of these changes, the source of energy was held in the hands. This is not very useful, for instance to leave home in a car released from a catapult would be both disconcerting and problematic – what would happen at traffic lights and in traffic jams? An on-board source of power is more convenient. To achieve this, the elastic band may be pinned at the front of the buggy and wrapped around the rear axle. When the axle is rotated, the elastic band is

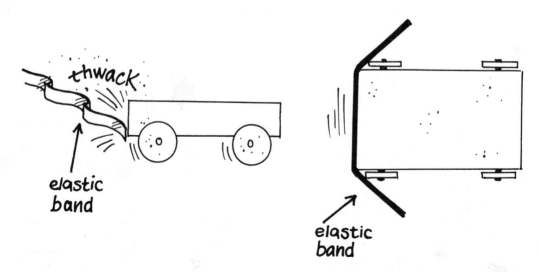

Figure 13.6 Two off-board ways of making a buggy move with an elastic band.

stretched so that there is something waiting to change. In changing, the wheels are rotated, which is just what is wanted.

Figure 13.7 On-board propulsion with an elastic band.

A spring is like an elastic band; when it is stretched, its length is waiting to change. When its length does change, it can provide a means of propulsion both off-board and on-board (Figure 13.8). Clockwork toys take advantage of this change.

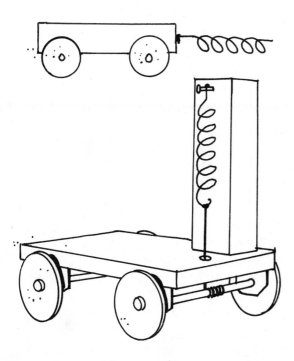

Figure 13.8 Off-board and on-board propulsion with a spring.

Gravity is also described as a source of energy. A weight on the edge of a table is waiting to change its position. If we help it to do so, it can be used to propel a buggy (Figure 13.9). As the weight falls in the gravicar, it pulls the string wrapped around the axle and rotates the wheels.

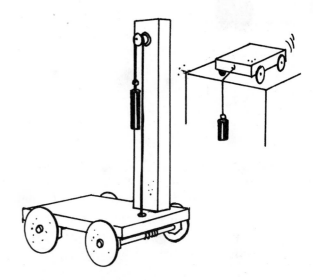

Figure 13.9 The 'gravicar' uses gravity for propulsion: off-board and on-board versions.

Children are usually familiar with battery-powered toys. Here, it is the chemicals that are waiting to change in the battery. As they change, electricity flows through the wires and makes the motor turn (Figure 13.10). The battery might look the same afterwards but that is only the outside. Inside, the chemicals are no longer what they were.

Figure 13.10 A battery-powered buggy

Batteries and people are much alike in this respect. A person looks much the same after a walk or a cycle ride as they did before it. Something useful was done but what has changed? It is, of course, the chemicals in the body that have changed; chemicals which had their origin in the food we eat.

Windmills obviously depend on the wind but, at first, it might not be clear what has changed in making the windmill do useful work. The wind, that is, moving air, can change; it can slow down or stop moving. As the wind turns the sails, its change is to slow down a little. This is also what happens when children blow a model land yacht along (Figure 13.11). Some toys use a so-called friction-drive to propel them. The child first pushes the toy vigorously to make a heavy wheel inside turn, then releases it to run under its own power. The spinning wheel is waiting to change. As it slows down, it propels the car along.

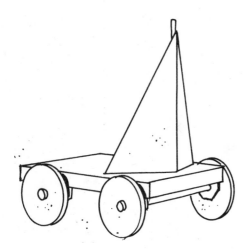

Figure 13.11 A model land yacht

There are many ways of organising things so that they are waiting to change. Stretching elastic bands and springs are mechanical ways of doing it; collecting materials into batteries, people, matches and gunpowder are chemical ways of doing it. Another way is to send pressure waves through air: we call it sound energy. If we make a material's molecules shake violently, we call it heat energy. In this way, there are a number of types of energy,

mechanical, chemical, heat, light, sound, electrical and so on. As they change, we can often make them do something useful.

Coal, gas and oil are known as fossil fuels because of their origin. These chemical sources of energy are limited in quantity. Other chemical alternatives, like wood and alcohol made from sugar cane, cannot, by themselves, make up any shortfall. They are, however, renewable. That is, they are made from plants that can be re-grown. The wind, waves, and heat and light from the sun are other sources of energy which might be tapped through wind generators, tidal power generators, solar furnaces and solar cells. There is also nuclear energy which arises from the arrangement of particles in the nucleus of the atom.

Energy is not often found in the form we want it. A piece of coal cannot be used to replace a dud battery, nor is a stretched spring useful to boil a kettle. Much ingenuity goes into changing one kind of energy into another. Coal burned in a power station is used to make steam which turns generators to produce electricity. Light bulbs are used to change electrical energy into light. Our bodies turn the chemical energy of food into heat, movement and electrical energy.

Energy can be measured and in fact, most homes will have meters which measure it. The scientific unit of measurement is called the *joule*, after the Victorian energy scientist, James Joule (1818–1889). The joule is a measure of how much is waiting to change, has changed, or is needed to effect a change. For instance, a jar of jam on the edge of a table, 1m above the floor, has available about 5 joules of gravitational energy. This becomes available if we let it fall and is very apparent if it falls on a foot. On the other hand, in contemplating a cup of tea on the same table, it is going to need about 1 joule of our chemical energy to lift it to the lips. An old-fashioned unit of energy is the *calorie*, still found in the slimmer's literature.

In technology, a source of energy and its controlled conversion into the required type is often an important consideration. In the classroom children meet this in a number of contexts such as making a working torch, making a model crane and making a self-propelled buggy. As was seen in one of the case studies in Chapter One, these are much more demanding tasks than is often realised. In making the self-propelled buggy, for instance, general experience seemed adequate for making the buggy but the rest defeated most of the children. They did not appreciate the nature of the problem, that something waiting to change *and* a mechanism for converting the change appropriately was needed. Not surprisingly, they were unable to pull these out of thin air. Experience over a period of time was needed in both science and technology of kinds, properties and uses of force and energy, and of *mechanisms* for using them.

An outline teaching scheme follows to illustrate the preparation needed. Note that in this scheme there is an interesting emphasis on on-board propulsion as time passes. The mechanisms useful for effecting on-board propulsion are experienced at

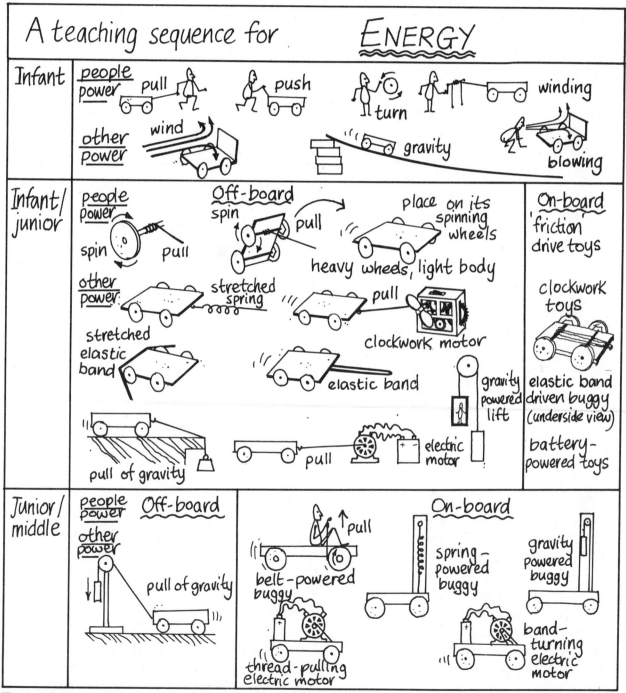

Figure 13.12 A teaching sequence for energy

earlier stages. Teaching should not be strongly didactic but rather more a guided discovery with an emphasis on direct experience. Each aspect needs to be presented in an interesting and relevant way. Sometimes, this might mean beginning with a toy and at other times it might be structured exploration (for example, how many ways can you make the wheels spin?); but on other occasions, there will be an investigation or a problem to solve.

Forces

Forces are pushes, pulls, bends or turns. A shopping trolley is usually pushed, while a shopping bag has to be lifted or pulled. Tree branches bend in a breeze and a pencil sharpener is turned or twisted. We are surrounded by forces, but we tend to take them for granted. Some are natural, like the force of gravity; others are applied in order to rearrange and control our environment. Rearranging materials into a form which satisfies a need and controlling them is a central concern of technology.

While we use a degree of force in shaping, moulding, cutting and joining materials, forces are consciously considered in the design of the product itself. Without this consideration a bridge, for instance, could be somewhat floppy. In a suspension bridge, the supporting cables are under tension and support the roadway, while in an old, hump-backed bridge, it is the piers which support the road and so they are under compression. Consider also a high, narrow van. On a tight bend, the force of gravity is likely to pull it over as it sways. This needs to be taken into account in the design. In making a buggy propelled by a elastic band, it becomes apparent that a thick band gives a large force and the buggy moves faster (see also **Energy**, page 176). Unfortunately, the large force also tends to make wooden wheels spin because the force of friction between them and the surface is often too small. This is usually solved by using other elastic bands as tyres for the wheels.

180

Force is measured in *Newtons*, after the seventeenth-century scientist, Isaac Newton (1642–1727). On the Earth, the force needed to lift a 100g mass is about 1N; for a 1kg mass, the force needed is about 10N. Force meters which measure the size of pushes and pulls in Newtons are available but can also be readily made from springs and calibrated with 100g masses.

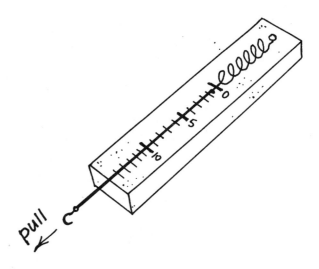

Figure 13.13 A force meter made from a spring. An elastic band can be used in place of the spring but it tends to weaken with age.

In the classroom, children need to experience the response of materials to different types and sizes of force and they should learn how to control and direct a force with simple mechanisms (see also **Mechanisms**, page 182).

Hydraulics

Hydraulic technology uses liquid pressure to transmit an effect from one place to another. Unlike air, confined water does not give way under pressure. Trapped in a pipe, a force at one end on a piston will be transmitted through the water to a piston at the other end. If the first piston moves, so will the second. If the second piston is larger than the first, it will not move as far, being able to accommodate more water behind the broader piston without great movement. However, as if to compensate for its smaller movement, it exerts a greater force. The same pressure spread over twice the area doubles the force. Although, as the title implies, water could be used as the liquid, in practical applications oil is used to reduce the risk of corrosion and freezing.

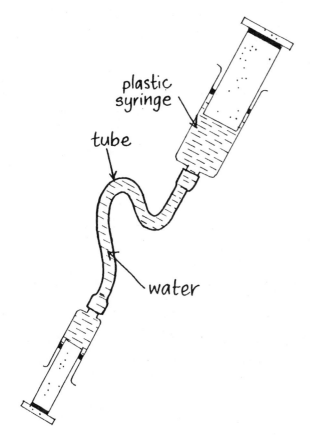

Figure 13.14 A large movement of the piston on the left gives a small movement of the piston on the right.

The most visible application of hydraulic technology is probably the mechanical digger, commonly used in building, road repairs and drain construction. The pipes carrying the oil and the bright piston rods can be seen clearly. Oil is pumped through the appropriate pipes to move the digger arm in the required direction. Hydraulic hoists and jacks are used in garages and the landing gear of aircraft is hydraulically operated. The brake pedal of a car is used to push in a piston in an oil-filled cylinder which transmits the pressure to pistons operating the brakes on the car wheels. The movement of robot arms used in the manufacturing industries is also effected by means of hydraulic technology.

The principles of simple hydraulics, like those of pneumatics, were known in the ancient world. Ctesibius of Alexandria designed a water clock which used the weight of water to turn various mechanisms. Water-wheels to tap the power of low pressure water supplies were commonplace in medieval Europe. High pressure devices would have been particularly difficult to make because of the problems of sealing a piston while leaving it free to move. Joseph Bramah solved this problem with a greased leather seal and was able to make an effective hydraulic press in 1795. In the nineteenth century, hydraulic cranes and passenger lifts were constructed and engines were run from the high pressure water mains.

In the classroom, a simple hydraulic device might be made from a balloon or plastic bag, a tube and a funnel. On pouring water down the tube, the pressure inflates the balloon or bag which might be used as a lift, jack or hoist. Two needleless plastic syringes, connected by a tube and filled completely with water, will show how a force exerted at one place can be transmitted to another. If the syringes are of different diameters, a difference in the magnitude of the transmitted force will be felt in an arrangement similar in principle to that of car brakes.

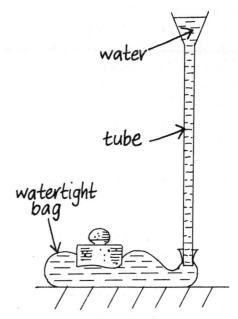

Figure 13.15a   Lifting a load with water.

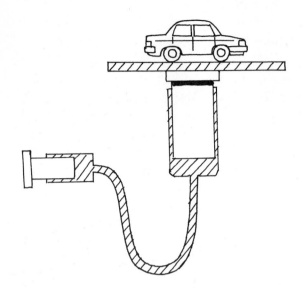

Figure 13.15b   Lifting a car hydraulically.

Materials

A material is that which is a part of the finished product. It may be a natural material, like wood or a synthetic material, like one of the plastics.

There are many ways of classifying materials. A materials scientist might sort them into metals, ceramics, plastics and composites, but what really matters is the properties of these materials; that is the basis on which they are selected. Some properties are readily determined by the senses: colour, transparency, weight and texture, for instance. Others are based on past experience or simple tests such as its response to cutting, to loads and impacts, to heat, to water and electricity, its strength, hardness, flexibility and elasticity. These are not always permanent, for instance some plastic bags become brittle after long exposure to sunlight, some carrier bags stretch permanently when loaded with heavy items, some metals corrode in damp air and many natural materials decay in a similar environment. However, some changes are desirable, as in a mixture of sand, gravel and cement, or when water is mixed with plaster of Paris, or when flour, yeast and water are heated.

182

In the classroom, children should widen their direct experience of the properties of materials and increasingly be able to discriminate between them. Materials should be classified in a number of ways according to their properties. Children's vocabulary needs to be steadily refined and made more precise. Many children use the single word *elastic* to mean an elastic band when the word really describes a property. There are lots of elastic materials, that is, those materials which return to their original shape when a load or force is removed. Wooden rulers and steel springs are more obvious examples, but even materials which are brittle often show some degree of elasticity. The children's attention can be drawn to the flexing of windows, the swaying of trees and the bending of aerials in a gale, all illustrating elasticity and, if the wind is strong enough, its limits. When choosing materials for a particular task, children need to answer questions of the following kind: Should it be smooth or rough? Should it be hard or soft? Should it be stiff or flexible?

Mechanisms

Mechanisms make it possible to have the kind of movement you want to create where you want it to occur. They may use one or more simple machines like the lever, the wheel and axle, the crank, the cam, the wedge, the pulley, the gear wheel and the screw. Mechanisms are often those crucial 'special' bits which make things work as intended.

A bicycle has a number of mechanisms: one for propulsion, one for braking and one for steering. The propulsion mechanism has cranks with pedals fitted to turn a toothed pulley wheel. The rotary motion is transmitted to the rear wheel via a chain and another toothed pulley on the hub. The braking mechanism uses a lever on the handlebars and a pair of levers astride the rim of the wheel. Linear movement of the handlebar lever is transmitted by a cable to the wheel levers which press brake blocks against the wheel's rim. Even the bicycle bell is a mechanism using simple machines. The kitchen also supplies many examples of mechanisms and the rotary whisk, the can opener, the hand-operated spray, the tap, the cupboard catch and the pedal bin are just a few.

The lever

The principle of the lever was first described by Archimedes in the third century BC, but levers have been used for thousands of years. At its simplest, the lever is little more than a pivoted rod. The position of the pivot determines the distance moved at the output end of the lever and the force needed at the input end. The crowbar and bottle opener are simple levers.

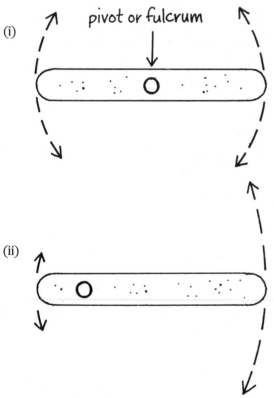

Figure 13.16 (i) Pivoted in the middle, the distances moved by the ends of the lever are equal. (ii) Pivoted near one end, the distances moved are not equal.

Often, one lever alone is insufficient to solve a problem. Two or more connected levers are known as *linkages*. The typewriter and piano depend on the action of linkages. Levers and linkages are very common in mechanisms.

Figure 13.17 Linkages used in a pantograph.

The wheel and axle

The wheel is designed to rotate. Often, as in a grindstone or bicycle, this is what is wanted: rotary motion producing rotary motion. Sometimes the rotation of a wheel is used to produce linear motion and sometimes linear motion is used to produce rotation.

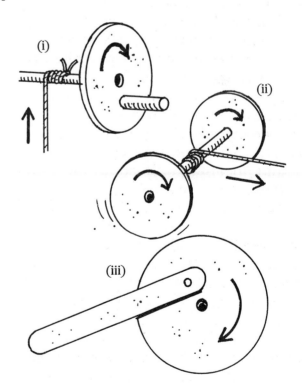

Figure 13.18 (i) Wheel, axle, and handle used to pull up a load.
(ii) A pull on the rope makes the wheels spin.
(iii) Moving the rod to and fro makes the wheel turn.

183

The crank

The crank is a wheel and axle with most of the wheel cut away and a convenient handle fitted.

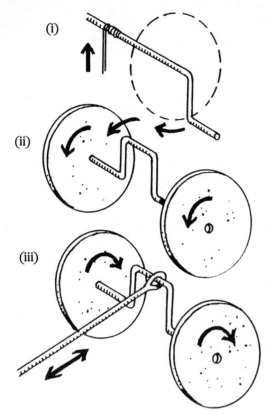

Figure 13.19 (i) The simple crank; compare with Figure 13.18 (i).
(ii) Wheels used to rotate a crank.
(iii) A rod used to make wheels turn *or* wheels used to make the rod move to and fro.

The cam

The cam is a non-circular wheel and axle. It can be used to produce linear motion from rotation.

Figure 13.20a   A toy with cam shaped wheels to make it waddle as it moves.

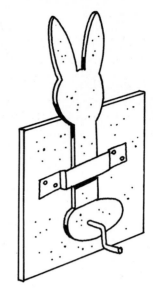

Figure 13.20b   A pop-up rabbit operated by a cam.

The pulley

A single pulley is a wheel and axle used to change the direction of a force or motion. Sets of pulleys make it easier to lift heavy loads or exert large forces, as in cranes and in a ship's rigging.

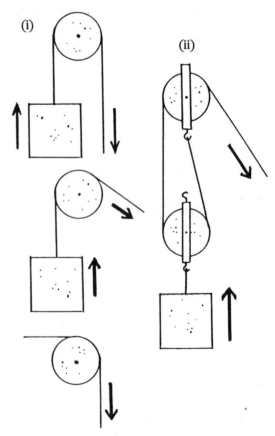

Figure 13.21 (i) One pulley wheel used to change the direction of the pull.
(ii) Two pulley wheels can make the task easier.

The gear wheel

The gear wheel is, in effect, a very rough wheel. When placed in contact with another, as it turns so must the other. Smooth wheels would do the same but would also tend to slip. Gear wheels are used to change the direction of rotation and, if necessary, the speed of rotation.

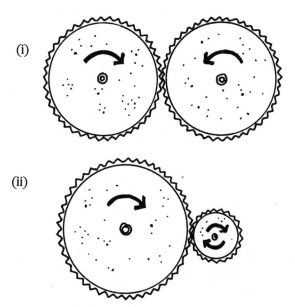

Figure 13.22 (i) One cog makes the other cog turn in the opposite direction.
(ii) A large cog turns more slowly than a small cog meshed with it.

Belt drives

To transmit rotation in one place to rotation in another, a belt might be used. In a washing machine, for instance, a belt from the motor drives the drum. Similarly, to use an electric motor to drive a buggy, an elastic band around the axle, stretched to the spindle of the motor, serves as a belt drive.

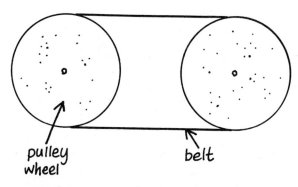

pulley wheel

belt

Figure 13.23 Two pulley wheels connected by a belt drive.

The wedge and screw

Climbing a hill using the long, shallow slope is easier than taking a path up the vertical cliff. A shallow incline makes the job easier. A wedge is a double-sided incline and it can be used to make tasks easier, too. Hammered into a log, it splits it easily.

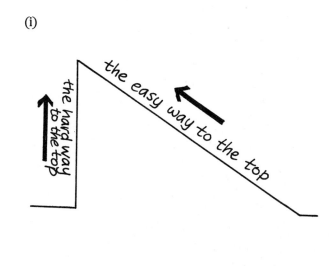

the hard way to the top

the easy way to the top

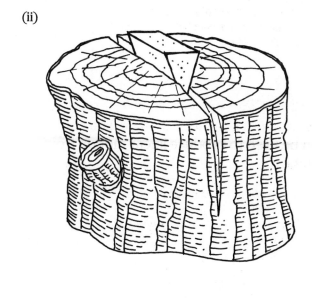

Figure 13.24 (i) The wedge-like incline is easier to negotiate than the vertical cliff.
(ii) A double-sided wedge makes it easier to split the log.

Sometimes, a road spirals to the top of a hill. This makes it like a long, shallow incline. A screw is like a rod with a spiral road wrapped around it and it can be used to make things move the way we want them to.

(i)

(ii)

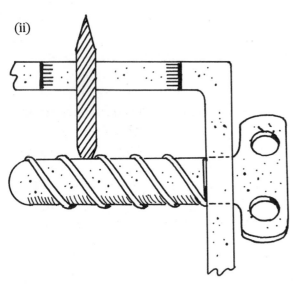

Figure 13.25 (i) A wedge-like incline wrapped around a hill.
(ii) The spiral arm on the key moves the pointer to and fro.

Return devices

Often, after a mechanism has been operated, it should return to its starting position ready to be used again. This is not required in the bicycle's steering mechanism, but it is in the braking mechanism and in the bicycle's bell. In both cases, this is brought about by a return

186

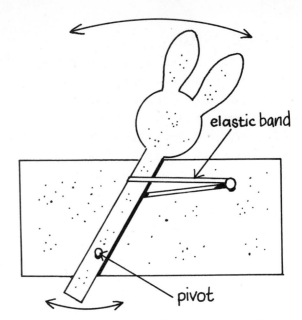

Figure 13.26 An elastic band as a return device.

spring. In other devices, a strip of springy steel is sometimes used. An elastic band or a bent strip of card may suffice in less permanent artefacts.

In the classroom, children should have the opportunity to use simple machines and mechanisms in their designs. It is unlikely that they will invent the basic units themselves so they need to see, use and try combinations of them, both in practical applications and in, for example, card or jelutong models or in kits. With this experience, they can begin to experiment to produce the motion they want to achieve.

Pneumatics

Pneumatic technology is the use of gas pressure to produce some desired effect. Often the gas used is air.

One of the simplest pneumatic devices is the drinking straw. The lungs reduce the pressure in the tube above the liquid and the surrounding air pressure pushes the liquid up the tube. A siphon depends on air pressure in a similar way. In these examples of pneumatic technology, the lungs are used to reduce the air pressure. In the vacuum cleaner, an electrical air-pump is used to reduce the air pressure above the carpet. The surrounding air rushes in through the carpet fibres, picks up dust and dirt and carries it into a porous bag. When we inflate a balloon, the lungs are used as a compression pump to increase the air pressure. The bicycle pump is a simple compression pump used to inflate tyres. A road drill works on compressed air delivered to it through a stout hose from a petrol or diesel driven compressor. Bus doors and automatic shop doors are operated pneumatically, the necessary difference in air pressure being supplied by the bus's engine and an electrical air pump, respectively.

(i)

air pressure

(ii) air pressure

Figure 13.27 (i) When some air is removed from the straw, the air pressure outside can push the water up it.
(ii) When air is removed from the siphon tube, the air pressure on the water pushes it through the tube.

The concept of pneumatic technology was known to the Ancients. Ctesibius of Alexandria designed a number of ingenious devices, among which was an organ operated by a reservoir of air which was kept under pressure by a foot pump. Hero,

also of Alexandria, continued in the same vein with a design for a whistling mechanical bird, operated by lowering a concealed bell into water to compress the air in the bell and thereby blow a whistle attached to it. The same effect can be produced by submerging the whistle of a kettle in a dish of water. In the nineteenth century, pneumatic technology became a more serious business. Telegram scripts and parcels were transmitted across London in carriers propelled through tubes by a difference in air pressure. In Paris and Pittsburgh, compressed air was supplied through pipes to factories to operate machinery and, also in Paris, trams carried reservoirs of compressed air to turn their engines and they 're-fuelled' from charging points at intervals along the track.

In the classroom, the lungs and the bicycle pump or foot pump are likely to be the main sources of safe, compressed air. Viscose tubing will serve to connect pump and appliance while balloons will act as air reservoirs. A jet propelled equivalent of the Paris pneumatic tram uses a balloon as a reservoir; a tipping truck uses the increasing bulk of stored air for lift. Needleless syringes, containing only air and connected by viscose tubing (see also **Hydraulics**, page 180), will transmit motion and may be applied in a number of ways. Used both in pneumatics and in hydraulics, they serve to illustrate the difference in the compressibility of air and of water.

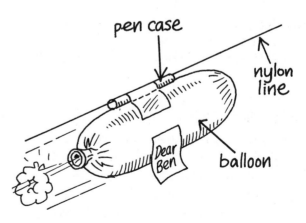

pen case

nylon line

Dear Ben

balloon

Figure 13.28a   Air pressure used to propel a message along a line.

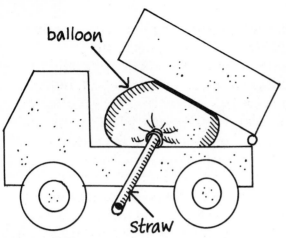

Figure 13.28b A tipping truck operated by air pressure.

Structures

A structure is an arrangement of materials intended to hold its form and to support, bear or withstand applied loads and forces. Structure is 'why things don't fall down' (J. E. Gordon, *Structures, or why things don't fall down,* Penguin, 1978).

We are surrounded by structures, both natural and man-made. In the plant world, the sturdy bulk of the tree trunk supports its branches, flowers are borne on tubes, hard shells protect nuts and leaves have ribbed skeletons. In the animal world, massive leg bones support heavy elephants, hollow, fused vertebrae make the bird's back rigid and shells guard flaccid snails. Each has its man-made counterpart: the massive bulk of the cathedral wall, the tubular steel chair, the crash helmet and the lattice work of a bridge.

Structures can be classified according to what they look like and what the forces in them do. A simple, what-they-look-like classification would be as follows.

Solid structures

A dry stone wall, concrete plinth or a dam, are essentially organised heaps of materials. For their strength, they rely on their bulk or their ability to withstand compression. Each block placed on the structure compresses those underneath. Many materials can withstand enormous compressive forces. However, if their cross-

section is not great, they may buckle and snap or shear, like wooden pit props under great loads. With metals this problem can be overcome by bracing it to give it a cross-section like the letter 'I'. Tubes may similarly be as effective as solid rods of the same diameter. This makes the structure strong, relatively light and reduces the amount of material needed. Bridging the gap between walls, however massive, can be a problem. If the roof is heavy, it might sag or collapse or push out the walls. A way of providing a roof so that its weight compresses the walls rather than pushing them out is a problem which has been faced by builders for at least a thousand years.

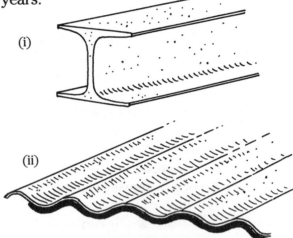

Figure 13.29 (i) An I-section girder. (ii) A sheet, corrugated for strength.

Shells

A shell is a curved, hollow structure which can bear a substantial load on its convex surface while a flat surface of the same thickness would collapse. On a convex surface the load compresses the material while on a flat surface, it stretches and fractures it. A dome, as used on a mosque, is one solution to the roofing problem.

Frames

Some structures such as triangular frames, are very strong. This makes them useful for making things where strength and lightness are essential. A bicycle frame, for instance, is made of tubes arranged in triangles. Often bridges and pylons are constructed similarly using rigid I- or L-section steel strips. When joints are welded, as in the bicycle, the frame becomes rigid. Bolted joints at the corners of frames can become slack so small triangles of sheet metal may be fixed there to increase rigidity. This technique is also used when working with jelutong in a structural approach which, to be precise, is really a framework approach to technology teaching.

The children's attention should be directed to structures in the natural and man-made world and they can be convinced of their utility by their designing and making in technology and their experiments in science.

Systems

A system is a set of connected units which operate together or interact to fulfil a need or achieve a goal. These units might be the ordered steps in a procedure or plan of action or they might be physical entities, each with its own contribution to make to the execution of the overall task.

As an example of a procedural system, consider the case of a business retailing toys. Without a procedural system, running this business could be inefficient and erratic. Each morning the mail arrives with a mixture of orders, payments for goods received and other categories of correspondence. Orders will go to the orders department where a check will be made on the status of the customer and the availability of the goods. All being well, the order and an invoice will pass from the orders department to the stores department. At the same time, copies will be sent to the accounts department. From the stores, the goods and invoice will pass to the packaging department and then to the despatch department. Among the incoming mail will be payments from shops for goods received. These will pass directly to the accounts department and then to the bank. If payment is not made after say, a month, the accounts department will issue another bill and inform the orders department of a change in the status of the customer. Each department performs a separate task. Performed in isolation, the tasks do nothing to achieve the goal but acting in concert, they do (Figure 13.30). In practice, a business may need several systems to perform its various functions and each of these might lock into the others in a grand, overall scheme. Of course, such systems do not just happen, they have to be designed.

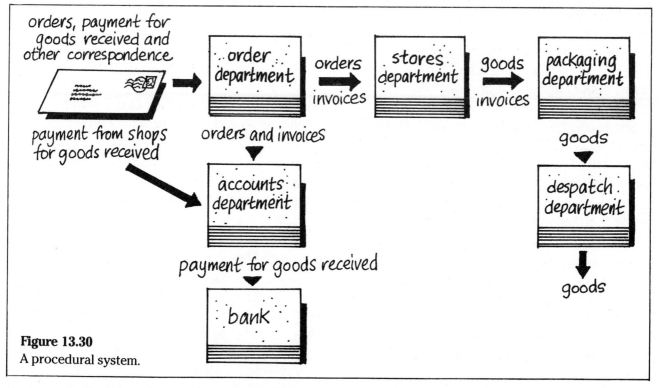

Figure 13.30
A procedural system.

Physical systems parallel procedural systems and each part is a 'department' with its own contribution to make to the objective. The bicycle, for instance, is a physical system with a propulsion department (pedals, chain drive, wheels), a steering department (handlebar mechanism), a stopping department (brakes), a storage-of-person department (seat), a lighting department (dynamo, front and rear lights), and a warning department (bell). Similarly, a kitchen is a system comprising areas for food storage, preparation and disposal. Each area alone does not make a kitchen but, taken together, they provide for the need for sustenance.

In the example of a business system, the mail was sorted and passed on and the orders department checked customer and stock. In other words, the order was *processed* in some way at each stage. Physical systems are capable of processing, too. The television signal, picked up by the aerial, will not give a picture and sound directly. The information in the signal must be sorted and amplified, that is, processed. Similarly, a coin sorter needs a unit where coins are poured in and then connects with a sorting device which, in turn, connects with a means of collecting the sorted coins.

Breaking down complex problems into manageable units according to function makes it easier to grasp what needs to be done (Figure 13.31). Of course, each of the units in a system may also be a system itself. Take, for instance, a pocket calculator. It needs a unit for us to feed in the information and give our instructions, a unit for carrying out those instructions, and one for presenting the result in a form we can understand. In reality, there is an input *system*, a processing *system*, and an output *system*. In such complex design problems, it is almost essential to look at the problem in terms of systems.

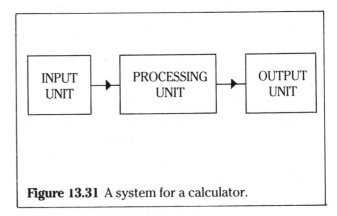

Figure 13.31 A system for a calculator.

An important aspect of technology is *control*. In the kitchen, the cook controls the process of food preparation. Without this *manual control*, too little, too much, or

inadequately cooked food might be produced. Similarly, in the business system (Figure 13.30), the accounts department monitors accounts and controls the flow of goods to customers.

It is very convenient when control is made *automatic*. The central heating system of a house uses automatic control to maintain an even temperature. It does this with a temperature sensor which passes its information to a processor. This checks to see if it is above or below a level set by the occupant of the house. If above that value, the central heating is turned off; if below, it is turned on. Here, sensors provide the input and the processor deals with it. This is an example of an *automatic control system*. The various parts act together to control the temperature in a house.

Separating the required action into units can make it easier to see what parts are needed and the relationship they have to each other. More complex control tasks may be rendered meaningful like this. For instance, a burglar alarm control system which is to be triggered only if the movement and the heat of a person is detected, might be as shown in Figure 13.32.

Figure 13.32 A system for a burglar alarm. Compare with Figure 13.4 (ii).

In the classroom, children need to learn what a system is by examining those that are familiar such as a lamp, a cooker, a kitchen, a bicycle and the computer (keyboard input, processor, monitor and printer output). In their own designing and making, they should look at some problems as simple systems and identify the components needed. This includes procedural systems like designing a routine to ensure that the preparation for some school event is organised. The children should examine examples of manual and automatic control, like the tape recorder and the ball valve of a water cistern, respectively. In procedural terms, control is often manual, being provided by the person in charge of the system.

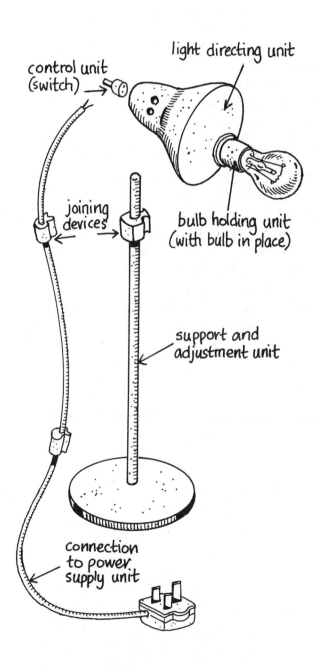

Figure 13.33 A lamp as a system for providing light when and where it is needed.

Bibliography

References

Ahlberg, J. and Ahlberg, A. (1989), *Burglar Bill*, Mammoth.

Association for Science Education (1990), *Teacher Assessment – Making it work for the Primary School*, ASE.

Blishen, E. (ed) (1963), *Oxford Book of Poetry for Children*, Oxford University Press.

Boswell, J. (1902), *Journal of a Tour of the Hebrides*, Macmillan.

Department of Education and Science (1985), *Science 5–16: A statement of policy*, HMSO.

Department of Education and Science (1988), *National Curriculum: First Report of the Task Group on Assessment and Testing*, HMSO.

Department of Education and Science (1990), Circular 3/90: *The Education Reform Act 1988: National Curriculum: Section 4 Order Technology*, HMSO.

The Design Council (1987), *Design and Primary Education: The Report of the Design Council's Primary Education Working Party*, The Design Council.

Ehlert, L. (1990), *Growing Vegetable Soup*, Gollancz.

Golden Eagle (computer package), Cambridge University Press (for 8–14 years).

Gordon, J. E. (1978), *Structures, or Why Things Don't Fall Down*, Penguin.

Hedderwick, M. (1986), *Katie Morag Delivers the Mail*, Picture Lion.

National Curriculum Council (1990), *Curriculum Guidance 3: The Whole Curriculum*, NCC.

Newton, D. P. (1990), 'Choosing Software – A Software Evaluation Schedule', *Information Technology and Learning*, 13(2), pp. 83–86.

Newton, D. P. (1990), 'Jack and Jill and the water problem', *Questions*, May 1990, 2(7), pp. 10–11.

Newton, D. P. (1990), 'An old woman faces up to the housing problem', *Questions*, 2(8), June 1990, p. 12.

Newton, D. P. (1990), 'My Fair Lady and the bridge problem', *Questions*, June 1990, 2(9), p. 13.

Newton, D. and Newton, L. (1990), *Bright Ideas Design and Technology*, Scholastic.

Reeves, J. (1967), *The Merry-Go-Round*, Puffin Books.

Rosen, M. and Griffiths, J. (1985), *That'd be Telling*, Cambridge University Press.

Schools Examination and Assessment Council (1990), *Guide to Teacher Assessment*, Heinemann Educational for SEAC.

Stobbs, W. (1983), *The House that Jack Built*, Oxford University Press.

Waters, D. (1987), *Primary School Projects*, Heinemann.

Williams, P. and Jinks, D. (1985), *Design and Technology 5–12*, The Falmer Press.

Other useful sources

Brooke, S. (1973), *Hearth and Home; a short history of domestic equipment*, Mills & Boon.

Dale, R. and Gray, J. (1979), *Edwardian Inventions 1901–1905*, W. H. Allen & Co.

Feldman, A. and Ford, P. (1979), *Scientists and Inventors*, Aldus Books.

Food Safety Advisory Centre (1991), *Food Safety: Your Questions Answered*, Food Safety Advisory Centre, 14 Soho Square, London, W1V 5FB.

Johnsey, R. (1990), *Problem Solving in School Technology*, Macdonald.

Kincaid, D. (1990), *An Early Start to Technology*, Macdonald.

Macauley, D. (1988), *The Way Things Work*, Dorling Kindersley.

Miller, N. (1989), *Edible Presents to Make*, Octopus-Hamlyn.

Penfold, J. (1988), *Craft Design and Technology: Past, Present and Future*, Trentham Books.

Readers Digest Books (1982), *The Inventions that Changed the World*, The Readers Digest Association Ltd.

Strandh, S. (1979), *Machines: An Illustrated History*, A. B. Nordbok, Gothenburg, Sweden.